DE LOREAN
Stainless Steel Illusion

by JOHN LAMM
Senior Editor, *Road & Track*
with commentary by former DMC executive Mike Knepper

$$\frac{N}{P}$$

THE NEWPORT PRESS

DE LOREAN
Stainless Steel Illusion

Editor: R.A. McCormack
Design Director: Paul Pfanner
  Pfanner+Catheron+Brown Design Inc.
Production: Anne Peyton
Typography: Alphabet Type
Printing: Times Printers Sdn. Bhd.

Newport Press ISBN 0-930880-09-9

Library of Congress card number 83-60220

Printed in Singapore.

Published by: The Newport Press
            1920 E. Warner Ave.   Suite M
            Santa Ana, CA   92705

Book trade distribution by:

Motorbooks International
Publishers & Wholesalers Inc
Osceola, Wisconsin 54020, USA

2

CONTENTS

Acknowledgements 4

Foreword 5

Prologue: *The Entrepreneur* 6

Chapter 1: *The Renegade* 16

Chapter 2: *Developing The Prototype* 22

Chapter 3: *The Serious Money* 46

Color Salon #1: *Styling & Prototypes* 57

Chapter 4: *Lotus Takes The Wheel* 66

Chapter 5: *Building The Factory* 78

Chapter 6: *"Star Wars" Assembly Line* 86

Chapter 7: *What John Hath Wrought* 94

Color Salon #2: *The Production Car* 113

Chapter 8: *Facing The Critics* 121

Chapter 9: *Coming Apart At The Seams* 130

Chapter 10: *The Aftermath* 142

Epilogue: *The Knepper Chronicles* 148

ACKNOWLEDGEMENTS

THE SCOPE OF this book has been through four stages that parallel the changing fortunes of the De Lorean Motor Company since early summer, 1981: apparent success, likely failure, success afterall?, failure. The first two men I contacted for the book were the same first two I met when I helped assemble the initial *Road & Track* story about De Lorean. That was early 1977, and Jerry Williamson was working out of C.R. "Dick" Brown's automobile dealership in Garden Grove, California, which doubled as DMC's West Coast office. A few weeks later *R&T*'s then-Engineering Editor, John Dinkel, and I met with Bill Collins at the DMC offices in Bloomfield Hills, Michigan. When Newport Press publisher R. A. McCormack and I decided to do this book in June, 1981, Williamson and Collins were the logical first contacts. Their help and encouragement have been invaluable.

The list of others who were helpful is long, and their aid and insight made the book possible. The DMC employees in the U.S. I talked with would have to begin with Mike Knepper, but also include Bruce McWilliams, C. R. Brown, Don Lander, Joe Black, Bob Dewey, Dave Woods, Steve Matson, and, of course, John De Lorean. At De Lorean Motor Cars Limited in Northern Ireland were Mike Loasby, Peter Moore and Shaun Harte. Not a De Lorean employee, but also from Northern Ireland is journalist Alan Watson Jr. of the *Belfast Telegraph*.

Mike Pocobello of Triad in Warren, Michigan was very helpful with his memories of the first prototype De Loreans, as were Mike Kimberley and Don McLauchlan of Lotus about the latter development stages. Dixon Hollinshead provided a great deal of insight into the building of the factory in Belfast.

Andy Weiss and Gene Daley of the West Coast De Lorean owners' clubs provided insight into what it's like to live with a De Lorean car. Jeff Pollack and Bruce Eide did the same from the salesman's standpoint.

Consolidated Industries' Sol Shenk, Linda Shafran and Jeff Abrams were very helpful about their company's involvement with the De Lorean.

And I must thank three of my colleagues: Karl Ludvigsen for his notes and thoughts on the entire De Lorean project; Otis Meyer, the *Road & Track* librarian, for his research help; and finally, Tony Hogg, for being someone I could talk to about the frustrations of the job.

It's a shame this book has become a post-mortem for the De Lorean Sports Car. I'm certain the men listed above who participated, despite their widely varied opinions about car and company, feel the same way. For myself, I must acknowledge the disconcerting feelings experienced during the course of the research and writing. These feelings were not caused by uncovering any devious activity. Rather, I kept encountering things which were never *quite* what they were billed to be. It led to the title of this book, i.e. illusion, "a perception that represents what is perceived in a way different from the way it is in reality." (Random House Dictionary of The English Language, unabridged edition, 1966.)

There was the perception of a safety vehicle, but the reality of a quite conventional car in this respect. A production automobile that *looks* like the prototype—but is totally different underneath. Carefree stainless steel that isn't. An ERM composite body that winds up conventional fiberglass. A De Lorean Sports Car by name—but a gull-winged Lotus in fact. Executive stock option plans that turned into zero options. Superb financing but questionable spending of $10 million a year on a Park Avenue office. The appearance of managerial harmony but the reality of deep resentments. Financial saviors who turned into phantoms—or worse.

The De Lorean Motor Company: one of the most dazzling feats in automotive history—and one of the most illusory. The perception of great promise and solid success, the reality of frustration and failure. *John Lamm*

FOREWORD

ALTHOUGH I HAD TALKED to John De Lorean on the telephone more than once, it wasn't until the spring of 1981 that I actually met him. The occasion was a visit I made to interview him at his ranch in Southern California in connection with a story I was writing for *Road & Track*.

My first impressions were that he was very tall, very handsome and very sensuous. He also appeared to be extremely confident, perhaps because it was at a time when the prospects for his company looked favorable, although he also seemed to be well aware of the risks he was taking with his project in Northern Ireland.

Actually, my visit was not really essential, because I had talked to many people about him and read a number of articles concerning him and his business, but I felt I needed to talk to him face to face. I didn't find the business tycoon that others found, but someone who appeared to be totally relaxed and surrounded by a happy family on the patio of a beautiful ranch house.

My immediate feelings were of awe and admiration for someone who had started with nothing and achieved so much in such a short period of time, and had plans for the future that bordered on the grandiose. I recall feeling, even at a time when things were going well, that his chances of success were probably less than 50/50, and if he was to be successful, the results would be entirely due to his own dynamism rather than to anything else. In fact, none of his critics could even have got the project off the ground.

Looking back, I think my main reason for wanting to meet De Lorean was to try to find out what drove him to take such risks, because what automobiles are really all about are automobiles and people, and the people are often more interesting than the automobiles they produce. After all, De Lorean had everything that money could buy and obviously money was not what drove him.

My conclusion was that when De Lorean left General Motors in 1973 at an early age and after great success, he did so because he had become just too big for General Motors and for some reason he was a bitter man. He still needed to prove himself and particularly to prove himself to the people at General Motors, and the only way he could do so was to build a better car than the Corvette because Corvette was a small enough operation to be open to competition.

Unfortunately, all De Lorean's efforts proved that it is now virtually impossible for anyone to enter the field of full scale car production with any chance of success—and I believe this to be true even in a healthy economy. Since World War II, about the only new companies to have succeeded are Porsche and Colin Chapman's Lotus. Chapman started with £25 borrowed from his wife-to-be and Ferdinand Porsche didn't start with much more. John De Lorean was fortunate in that he started with sufficient funds and guarantees to succeed—if success was possible. However, all Colin Chapman had to lose was £25, John De Lorean brought a lot more to the table. This was partly due to the gullibility of the British Socialist party that was in power at the time. If the Conservative party had held the purse strings the situation would have been different. Though Mrs. Thatcher must have seen in De Lorean a person as strong and dynamic as herself, she probably wouldn't have given him a red cent, for she is extremely hard nosed as far as the British taxpayers' money is concerned.

I ended my story for *Road & Track* by saying, ". . . even if success should prove elusive, one can rest assured that the world will not have heard the last of John Zachary De Lorean." Unfortunately, I was right.

When the whole affair came to an end with the arrest of De Lorean, I was sorry, very sorry, because I hate to see failure. Not only was I sorry for De Lorean, but also for those people in Northern Ireland who had never had a job before, and will, in all probability, never have one again. *Tony Hogg*

PROLOGUE:

The Entrepreneur

A S THIS IS WRITTEN John De Lorean's motorcar company lies in ashes and he awaits trial for allegedly financing an enormous cocaine deal. A tragic ending and an ugly accusation. Hardly the ending envisioned when the research for this book began 18 months ago. It was to be the story of a dream car come true, an adventure in advanced engineering and skillful marketing, an inspiration for those who believe they have a better idea—maybe proof to the world that America is still the land of opportunity, even if the hero is pulling himself up by his Gucci bootstraps.

The reactions to John De Lorean's arrest and subsequent indictment for drug trafficking have been varied in tone, but consistent in puzzlement. Why did he do it? There were lots of answers. Many in Britain felt it was the unmasking, the swindler exposed, the con man cut down by his greed. Yet many of his closest associates, men who had worked with him for years and who might be expected to smile knowingly, were stunned. Many of us, whether journalist, car enthusiast, or star enthusiast, no doubt felt a little older, a bit more cynical and disillusioned on hearing the news. We wanted to believe, we wanted success, we wanted him to win! We felt let down, almost betrayed—he must have broken under the stress, he must be crazy. Why else would he allegedly engage in a criminal act, he who had the whole key ring to the good life, he who wanted to build the "ethical" car. He must have slipped off the edge.

Let's Ask An Expert

Just what kind of man is John De Lorean? We asked psychologist Dr. Keith Golay* if he would try

and give us an answer—to try and provide some insight as to why a man would do something so apparently out of character. For that matter to try and give us some better handle on a man who has been described as enigmatic, and whose behavior seems full of contradictions. On the one hand he has stated he cares nothing for money, and yet on the other there are law suits and accusations of real estate improprieties and questionable business deals.

He is extremely wealthy and acquisitive, insists on nothing but the best, "would rather be sterilized than go second class"—and yet professes his work is all that really matters to him, publicly thumbs his nose at $650,000 per annum and takes the most famous hike since the Duke of Windsor turned in his coronation costume. The man who derided the morality of GM executives, who sold his interest in the San Diego Chargers professional football team because he felt the alleged use of drugs on the team set a poor example for the youth of America, has been arrested for allegedly investing $1.8 million with a cocaine dealer to raise money to save his company.

Q: *What makes John De Lorean tick? He almost appears to fit the hoary cliché of the "split personality." Is he schizoid? Has he flipped? He has clearly demonstrated the classic reaction of the besieged executive who gradually withdraws and cuts himself off from his trusted advisors, cloaking himself in a mantle of imperviousness and trusting only himself. Is this the same engineer who climbed the stairs at General Motors faster than anybody ever has before or since?*

A: Well, first of all I don't think he's "crazy." On the contrary, after wading through all that back-ground material and confirming my suspicions with interviews I feel his behavior is quite consistent with his personality type, and those apparent contradictions are readily explained.

---

*For some background on Dr. Golay and the psychology of personality types, see pg. 10

John De Lorean radiates the confidence and style for which he is famous in this 1978 photo taken in his Park Avenue office.
(Terry Ashe)

Chubby-cheeked early days at GM...　　　*New Pontiac leader, new face...*

Q: *This is a bit surprising. I didn't think things would be so neat and tidy . . .*

A: I didn't say it was going to be neat and tidy. First of all, this is a complex man, a genius really, and to understand this type of man you have to recognize that great actions never come from stable, satisfied states. They only come from an inner drive and restlessness. Anybody who exhibits the kind of genius De Lorean does at organizing and influencing people is doing so only because he is forced to do so. This is a very important concept to hang on to as we push along in our discussion. Inner tensions are driving him constantly to new output. De Lorean recognized this about himself when he said, "You know, I really don't know why I'm the way I am, but I have this force that pushes me—and I don't think that's a very good way to live." This force, this drive, stems partly from his upbringing, coming from a working class family.

There are other components to this drive, however, that are just as important. Without constantly renewed *risk* life has no charm for him, so he seeks stimulus from playing for high stakes. He's almost contemptuous of prolonged contemplativeness. He talked about leaving GM saying he did so because he felt he was "in the stands and not playing the game anymore. It's my nature to run. I live on adrenalin." His skills as a manager are much more akin to the audacious tactics of a General Patton rather than some carefully thought-out strategy. The way he manages is instinctive.

Q: *He said he believed in hiring good men and letting them do their job. Apparently he was able to hire plenty of good men, but there is ample testimony now of unhappiness in the executive suites both in the U.S. and Northern Ireland because he would meddle and not let people do their job.*

A: This is because he always wants to be where the action is and he makes impulse decisions based on what he perceives at the moment needs to be done. But this action isn't planned out, or based on some carefully thought out analysis of how to solve the problem.

Q: *Sounds like you're drawing a textbook portrait of the entrepreneur, like William C. Durant for instance, who once he gets the ball rolling and the ship moving is drawn to a new project . . .*

A: On to where the action is. He's not interested in preservation. But—when there's a problem—he's there. Problem solving, dealing with crises—that's exciting. The entrepreneur is usually superb at solving crises, except that he tends to make decisions in an *impulsive* manner, and that can result in poor decisions when you need to weigh the relative consequences of an event.

Q: *Okay, so we have the entrepreneurial aspect of John De Lorean's personality . . .*

A: Yes, but probably one of the greatest entrepreneurs of our time. Anybody who can gather together nearly $200 million of other people's money—gaining the confidence of the kind of people he did—is a master. The operative word here is confidence. Gaining and preserving that confidence—*both in terms of how he sees himself and how others see him*—is what motivates John De Lorean. He lives and thrives on this confidence. *That's* what people call his "charisma." His physical type—tall, handsome, stylish—matches his personality type in a way that is . . . well, I'm afraid there's no other word for it—unique.

This is a guy who is so acute in his observations of sensory phenomena he can tell what a man wants to hear, what a man *needs* to hear in order to move that person in the direction he—De Lorean—wants him to go.

Q: *Does he consciously do this?*

A: Well, it's more of a complete sensory awareness. He's tuned in to the cues other people give him—both

Maverick on the 14th floor...   *On his own at last at DMC... (Ashe)*

verbal and non-verbal—and he has the ability to interpret those cues, use this input, to gain the confidence of others. For example, I would bet he didn't have a detailed, systematic plan that would *prove* he could successfully build his company. It was his charismatic manner and his track record people invested in.

Q: *Well the SEC would probably agree with that in view of the disclaimer they made them read at the beginning of each one of the dealer presentations. Okay. Now,* People *magazine raised the question of why De Lorean was vulnerable to the cocaine trade and its promise of euphoric profits. Certainly he was desperate to save his company, but does that explain*

it? What about another person who might find himself in a similar situation? There are plenty of businesses in trouble today whose owners aren't dialing up the local drug distributor.

A: Different people react differently under the same conditions. What we need to look at to understand his action is his core personality, and not get confused or distracted by all the branches on the tree. We can come up with hundreds of traits, a long list of likes and dislikes and still not grab the essence of what this man's about. What we need to look for is his personality *type*—what leads him to certain ways of thinking, emoting and acting. A theme if you will, a thematization.

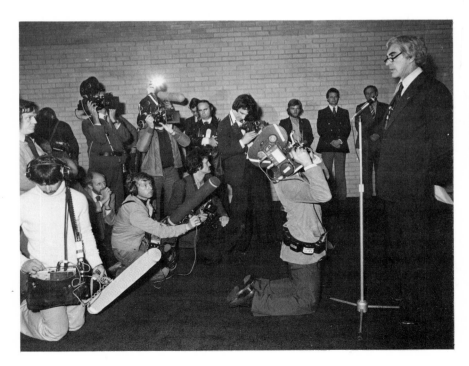

Speaking at the press conference following groundbreaking for the factory in Dunmurry on Oct. 2, 1978, De Lorean has full command of the media event. (DMC)

PSYCHOLOGICAL TYPES

Dr. Keith Golay and The Science of Typology

Dr. Keith Golay (Decruyenaere)

Dr. Keith Golay, 38, is a Professor at California State University (Fullerton campus) where he trains marriage, family and child therapists, as well as school psychologists. In addition he maintains his own clinical practice, and has just published his first book, "Learning Patterns & Temperament Styles" (Manas-Systems, Newport Beach, CA, 1982).

Dr. Golay specializes in the science of typology, or personality types, and is a colleague and associate of Professor David Keirsey, whose work is among the best known in the field. Keirsey is the co-author, with Marilyn Bates, of "Please Understand Me" (Prometheus Nemisis Books, Del Mar, CA, 1978). Keirsey in turn bases his unifying systems approach on the pioneering identification of personality types through testing accomplished by Isabel Myers (Myers-Briggs Type Indicator, published by Consulting Psychologists Press, Palo Alto, CA). The fundamental idea of psychological types is of course the work of Carl Jung.

The overriding emphasis in Dr. Golay's work is the study and understanding of "natural" as opposed to "pathological" behavior. This is a critical distinction. Dr. Golay has also extensively analyzed prison as a social system in an attempt to determine why prisons don't seem to correct criminal behavior but instead preserve and in many cases exacerbate this behavior—psychological case experience which is, regrettably, of value in this profile.

With increasingly sophisticated testing methodology, a coherent theory of psychological types is helping to resolve some of the apparent conflicts and internecine warfare which have raged in the field of psychology ever since Adler squared off against Freud. Generally speaking, psychologists and psychiatrists regard behavior as purposive, i.e. man is a motive-bound creature. There have been any number of powerful arguments put forth as to just what that instinct, or motive or purpose might be. Freud believed we were all driven by pleasure, thus satisfying our sexual instinct. Adler said uh-uh, we are all seeking power, trying to overcome our feelings of inferiority. Sullivan put it all down to a craving for social solidarity. And Abraham Mazlow has us seeking self-actualization.

Rather than attempting to find one motive driving us on which we all share in common, Jung, Myers and now Keirsey conclude each of us is driven by a *different* motive. Certain people are predisposed to one motive and certain people to another. Keirsey adds in another idea to unify the whole approach, the less-mystifying concept of self-esteem as opposed to the vague urgings of instinct. So, there are some of us who like ourselves better when we live spontaneously, some hold themselves in higher regard when they achieve social belonging, others feel better as their powers increase, etc. Keirsey, then, is interested in observing, classifying and understanding human *differences,* and describes different personalities in terms of total behavior patterns—from which he has distilled 16 specific types.

In applying his knowledge of personality types to John De Lorean, Dr. Golay has had access to the research of author John Lamm, and conducted in-depth interviews with De Lorean associates Mike Knepper and Bruce McWilliams, both former top executives with the firm. Editor R. A. McCormack of The Newport Press wrote the opening remarks and conducted the interview.

Johnny Carson's half-million dollar investment in the dream will now only yield wry wisecracks on the "Tonight" show, but this shrewd Midwesterner is an excellent example of just how successful John De Lorean was at winning the confidence of important people in all walks of life. (DMC)

Q: *But will that tell us why he allegedly broke the law to try to save his business?*

A: Ultimately, yes, it will lead us to the answer. For now, however, let's establish that one of the crucial qualities of his personality type is his need to gain the confidence of other people. He hungers to have personal impact on people. He sees himself as confident and wants others to see him the same way. The question is, what makes him so extraordinary at being able to gain other's confidence?

Q: *What is your answer?*

A: He's the kind of man who has tireless energy, is mentally sharp, daring, unshackled. He is eloquent. His perception of the moment is lightning quick. He's the kind of guy, as I said a bit earlier, who observes the man he's to deal with, determines the real possibilities and uses whatever "language" he needs to make people feel comfortable.

There are loads of examples of this in previously published interviews going back many years. He vowed to start the "ethical" car company and gave illustrations of how the other companies were unethical. He expressed a desire to give jobs to people who were out of work; he said, "God stuck me here to be part of the solution." He aligned himself with Jesus in a very ingratiating, almost mystical way, saying, "In many ways Jesus was an outsider, he was a radical. Some of the big things in life are achieved by those who refuse to conform. I'm an outsider."

Okay, now—on the one hand he says things that make people feel confident in him—but on the other he does what he wants to do. He says he believes in the Ten Commandments, yet he has a history of questionable business dealings. Dewey [Bob Dewey, former De Lorean financial officer] has that wonderful quote in the *LA Times* where he says De Lorean "suffered from moral anemia." De Lorean says things to gain people's confidence—not because he believes in it

himself. This is the ultimate pragmatist, the ultimate realist. He focuses on the reality of what he needs to do to get what he wants. That's why he invented the phantom investors—he knew that's what people wanted to hear.

Q: *John Lamm, in his interviews the past year or so with De Lorean executives, discovered—with some discomfiture—that De Lorean exhibits a pattern of taking people in, getting the most out of them, using them up, getting rid of them, and then if they ever say one word about it—labeling them turncoats.*

A: Right, yes. That's a maneuver, a tactic. Politicians are very good at it too, disqualifying the opposition. The name of the game is to get people on your side, to persuade them using whatever means are at hand. De Lorean's not *for* morality, he's not *against* morality—that's simply not an issue. Morality has nothing to do with pragmatism—it's whatever works.

Q: *Doesn't that make him a sociopath?*

A: No. People with a different temperament may see this behavior as irresponsible, but they have a different perspective than he does.

Q: *Hold on . . . that "No" was a fast and unequivocal answer. Why is he* not *a sociopath? A sociopath in my understanding is a person who does what he wants to do to further his own ends and has no conscience regarding his acts . . .*

A: That's a definition given to this type of personality by a *different* type of personality. It's arbitrary. But is it really true? No. He's responding in a way that's natural to him.

Q: *I'm sorry, I'm afraid I can't be that sanguine about it, because now he's allegedly responded in a criminal way . . .*

A: Yes, right, his behavior became unproductive. He himself got conned by the easy buck, the fast buck. Plus the *risk!* He's a guy who *knows* what risk is. He knows you've got to take a risk if you're gonna make

11

it big and he needed to make it big real quick. Also his associates all described him as a man with ice-water in his veins. The guy never got nervous, never worried, he was cool, calm and collected even in the most heated debate—even when he was arrested! He's *not like* the average man who gets upset by things. He gets off on crises, on exciting circumstances.

Q: *Apparently the ice water was running a little warm when he was dealing with the British receivers and trying to talk to his dealers this past summer. There were reports he was flustered and repeated himself and didn't seem to be all there . . .*

A: Exactly—he began to lose their confidence. Like anyone else with certain deep personal needs, as you begin to lose that which you need . . . it's like food . . . as you begin to use up what's there and you're not getting the input you need . . . the energy . . . then the system starts to deteriorate.

Q: *So in a very real sense what you're saying is that having other people's confidence is a source of energy for John De Lorean . . .*

A: Yes. Take a respected man in the community who loses his job for some reason. He runs out of money, he's starving, he needs food. For survival he steals a loaf of bread. What's the morality of that? The important thing to remember is that psychic hunger is just as real, as driving—it needs to be fulfilled just as physical hunger does.

Q: *You've referred several times to De Lorean as a personality "type." Just what "type" is he?*

A: Well, Myers & Briggs have described this type as the ST, the sensory, thinking. David Keirsey's Temperament Theory, which is the most current description of personality types, would describe De Lorean as the Extroverted, Sensory, Thinking, Perceptive—the ESTP. This is the promoter, the organizer.

Q: *Is De Lorean a good example of the ESTP type?*

How well does he fit the mold?

A: He is probably the finest example I've ever come across.

Q: *What are some of the characteristics of the ESTP?*

A: This type of person sees life as having an unending supply of resources. Life is to be lived day to day and its resources are to be used. De Lorean even used the cliché, "You only pass this way once." Having the best of everything, going first class, that's typical of this person. They know how to enjoy life.

Resourcefulness is another critical hallmark of the ESTP—and De Lorean personifies that capability. This has to do with an ESTP's ability to use the sensory cues in his environment to solve problems in the here and now. Excitement is another characteristic. This type of person lives for excitement. We've already noted De Lorean admits he thrives on adrenalin.

Q: *If in 20 years another perfect specimen of the ESTP arrives on the scene, is he too going to wind up under indictment?*

A: If he doesn't clearly realize his own limitations maybe so. Once he leads people to where he wants to go, he needs to turn things over to somebody whose strength is his weakness. He needs somebody who can plan systematically and design systems to accomplish the tasks ahead.

Q: *A lot of successful people seem to have massive egos, but also a touch of humility as well, helping them to know their limitations. Is De Lorean a victim of his ego?*

A: You sometimes hear the word "ego-maniac" used to describe De Lorean, but I disagree. I don't think that's what he is at all. I don't think he separates the "I" from the rest of the world. On the contrary, he and the outside world are one. What people see as self-love or self-indulgence does not to me seem an abrupt setting up of himself against the outside world. He knows what he's capable of. He believes he can move

mountains. He swims confidently in the world. He's tuned in to the world and thoroughly enjoys it; he takes advantage of it and it gives him a feeling of confidence *because* he's so in tune. It's very much like driving a race car. For the really good driver he and the car are one—he *knows* he can negotiate that next curve ahead. I think De Lorean feels this way about the world he lives in—he and the business world are one.

Q: *That's a pretty good analogy. I guess that's why we can feel so acutely sad when a great driver like Jim Clark or Gilles Villeneuve is killed, even though we never so much as shook his hand . . . They paid with their lives for their greatness, for their oneness with the machine. Hardly fair . . .*

A: They pushed it to the nth degree, always testing the limit, always going all the way. If you think that you and the car and the environment are one, if you really believe that—what can happen, what can go wrong? That's what allows this ESTP type to make the breakthroughs and accomplish the things they accomplish. If you're afraid, nervous, worried—you can't do it.

Q: *So, Jim Clark and Gilles Villeneuve paid with their lives and now John De Lorean may pay with a jail sentence . . .*

A: He'll pay for it the rest of his life. You see he won't ever be able to regain the level of confidence that he needs. That will be disastrous for him. I don't think he'll stop making deals or get out of the game— but he won't continue playing on the same level. He reached the peak, he's been king of the mountain and it's unlikely he'll get back to the top. But he'll still be living in the fast lane.

Q: *How was it—as an ESTP—that he was able to function so brilliantly in a highly disciplined, planning-oriented bureaucracy such as General Motors?*

A: He excelled at GM precisely because of that acute awareness of what people wanted. He designed a car that exactly matched what people wanted at the time [the Pontiac GTO]. The others at GM really weren't in tune with what the populace needed or wanted. De Lorean is able to solve problems not through using principles or abstractions but through very pragmatic, concrete solutions.

The way he *uses* his intelligence is very different from say, an Einstein, who might spend all day studying how to screw in a light bulb. For an Einstein concrete issues are irrelevant. De Lorean's is a practical intelligence, a genius at organizing, promoting—a genius entrepreneur. But not a genius like Einstein; the two are polar opposites in temperament theory.

One of the problems with the perceived image of De Lorean is that by education and occupation he's an engineer, and we all tend to see engineers in the stereotype of the slide rule. The slide rule representing abstractions, theoretical models. There's another kind of engineer—the practical engineer, who knows what exists in the real world and how to make it work. To ask him to come up with a plan for how to get a man to Mars and back—no way, it's theoretical, it doesn't exist in the real world. But ask him to design a spaceship that meets specific criteria based on a concept and he could do that. He knows what can be done with the concrete, with the practical. He's a realistic painter, not an abstract expressionist.

Q: *ESTP's are fairly rare birds, I would imagine?*

A: Thirteen percent of the population actually. But to find them in high places in management or the professions *is* unusual, because this requires that they get a lot of advanced education. They bomb out early in school because they don't like to study—they want hands on experience. Fortunately, some of them, like De Lorean, wind up at technical institutes. But I'll bet he didn't ace the theoretical math courses.

Q: *Did his working class background help propel him, help motivate him to stay in school?*

A: Probably. He wanted to overcome the deficit, because he wants to enjoy, to seize all the good things in life. He mentions how Bunky Knudsen introduced him to the finer things in life. Overcoming the lack of resources in his early life helped fuel his inner drives. At GM he began to see the possibilities.

Q: *Is it fair to say that rather than undergoing a transformation at GM it was more of a fulfillment? That he began to achieve the possibilities, but when he was promoted out of the action position that's why he left?*

A: Yes, it's a fair statement. Gail Sheehy in *Passages* brings that out very clearly. She says, "De Lorean's restlessness was intensified by his promotion to corporate vice president. It deprived him of his showcase as a star division manager. Where he had run his own show he now found himself in a decompression chamber. He was an isolated group executive."

Q: *What's the difference between a con man, pretending certain things for his personal gain, and De Lorean? Is there no pretend?*

A: No pretend. That's what life *is* to John De Lorean. It's taking advantage of all the resources that exist and using them in the game of life—because you only go through once. Live and let live is his attitude. Enjoy it while you can.

We need these kind of people though—daring, clever, quick, resourceful. These are the people who make things happen, constantly pushing forward, testing the limits. Of course once the deal's together someone else should step in and manage it.

Q: *Why is it De Lorean was unable to see that? We're talking about a man who is very bright, the ultimate pragmatist, who puts together a fabulous financial deal to get his company going, but who can't see he'd be better off to bring in the planners and the good grey-faced managers to manage it for him.*

A: He thought he needed to do everything himself to make sure he didn't lose. It's like asking someone else to play your poker hand. He also focuses on the short term, the here and now, and there were constant short term fires to put out and battles to win. Remember that the GTO was based on an existing car to which De Lorean had them add an existing big engine and *bang*—it was all done. Moment to moment he's convinced that with the right amount of money problems can be solved. Time was working against him however, as the bottom dropped out of the economy.

Q: *What about the key decision made in November to double production in the face of his advisors' objections?*

A: From what I understand he had to take a gamble, try and raise some money by selling more cars. Again, I think it was probably an impulsive decision, because from what I read this decision actually cost the company some $22 million to do. [DMC executive C.R. Brown made this comment—Ed.] Put a person in the position of having to now prove what they've conned everybody into and they've got to come through with the goods—and he knew it. Everybody was looking at him, the eyes of the world were on him. That's a lot of pressure. Even with nerves of steel he's going to feel the stress. As the stress mounts he relies increasingly on his own processes, his self-confidence, his own personal track record of problem solving. In my opinion the people around De Lorean could not present their objections in a manner to reach him.

Q: *What about the comment that he was enigmatic, that you couldn't get close to him?*

A: Closeness has no relevance to De Lorean. He's not concerned with closeness. He's a pragmatist, this is a business deal. Plus it's part of mystifying people, part of staying "one up."

Q: *What about this raging contradiction between De Lorean stating, "I never worry about money, I do things for themselves," contrasted against the opulent*

lifestyle, the Concorde jet flights, the Claridges in London, the huge salary.

A: When you play Monopoly you're supposed to buy as many pieces of property as you can. That's what the game is all about. That's the way the ESTP sees life. He treats money as unimportant. He doesn't hoard it, he's not a pennypincher. In fact, De Lorean really *doesn't* believe money is important. Money is simply another of life's resources that you acquire and use. It's a vehicle, nothing more. Money doesn't have innate value for him. It has no sentimental value, like baby pictures. To him there's always more where that came from. Life's full of money. Why worry about money when it's all around you? It's unimportant. What's important is the game, the action, the excitement—the getting and spending. Having it is irrelevant. De Lorean knows about life's possibilities. Money is there for the taking, like walking into a candy store, stepping up to the counter and getting what you need.

Q: *Even though De Lorean may view life as one big candy store, I'm still having trouble accepting the fact that a man of his achievement would allegedly cross the line and engage in criminal activity . . .*

A: Well, think of it in terms of match-ups. What keeps most of us on the straight and narrow? 1) Fear, 2) It will make me feel guilty, and 3) I'll get nervous as hell and fall to pieces while attempting it. Now, take a look at De Lorean. He's got nerves of steel, he knows how to maneuver within a high risk environment, and he doesn't have a conflict morally because to the ultimate pragmatist you do whatever works.

If you look at his personality type you can see how he would in fact fall prey to this kind of behavior; it's not difficult to envision. He was desperate to preserve his self-confidence, to maintain the confidence of others—to replenish his food supply. He was willing to take the risk. In fact I believe one of the under-

cover agents was quoted as saying that De Lorean was exhilarated by the whole thing, that it turned him on. If you or I were trying to pull something like that off we would have been so scared and nervous about the consequences we'd have had diapers on under our shorts. For De Lorean the consequence is just one more challenge to overcome and deal with . . . a challenge to beat the system, to win this game.

Q: *I think he's already taken the first step by striding out of Terminal Island with a Bible in his hand. Any closing comments?*

A: Yes. I would like to ask that we all look at John De Lorean in the context that people are different. Each of us views De Lorean through our own prism, based on *our* personality type. Part of the problem is that we all tend to think everybody is like ourselves—or should be. The person who's not like us? Well, maybe there's something wrong with him. He's a deviant. We're all quick to pass moral judgment, to write people off.

It's possible John De Lorean has committed a criminal act, and no one can support such an act. A more meaningful question for us all to ponder is not whether he did or didn't, but who is this person and how do we understand him? Better understanding on our part of an entrepreneurial genius like John De Lorean, better understanding of *any* human resource, could help us prevent some of them from self-destructing.

1

The Renegade

I REMEMBER ONCE IN 1969 making a short cut around the Chevrolet Engineering building at the GM Technical Center in Warren, Michigan specifically to get a look at the Chevrolet Caprice limousine John De Lorean ordered built so he could ride around in more style. He was head man of Chevrolet, at 44 the youngest General Manager to ever hold the post. But his idea of style didn't match up with the corporate brass, and they ordered the car destroyed. Three years later De Lorean made his now-famous stage right exit from the 14th floor, the equally well-known stratum housing GM's top corporate executives, among whom De Lorean was supposedly the heir apparent to the throne. Members of the media may have been doing most of the supposing, because by then he had become good copy. Whether he quit, or was in fact asked to leave by President Ed Cole is still a matter of conjecture, but he certainly didn't leave in disgrace. Indeed GM took some pains to see that he obtained a job as head of the National Alliance for Businessmen, and in fact paid the $200,000 salary that came with the position. (Rumors persist to this day about the "real" reasons for his departure. But none of his detractors has been willing to step forward with name, rank and serial number, and the corporate office has never shown the slightest interest in disagreeing with De Lorean's version of why he left.)

It is here that our story begins, when conjecture ends and the saga of the De Lorean Motorcar Company starts to take shape, because John De Lorean didn't move from his executive halfway house in the National Alliance to some new position of real corporate power. It was more of take-this-job-and-shove-it on a truly grand scale…"I was offered the chairmanship of a major company with tremendous stock options and everything else, which would have been a very easy life. Looking at the stock today (1982) my interest would have been worth about $21 million—

and all I had to do was sit there."

GM's corporate leaders knew what he was really up to, however, for they had put a clause in his contract forbidding him from working for another automotive company after his departure, upon penalty of forfeiting handsome bonuses he was scheduled to receive in the future. Not that GM was worried about the competition, but why help finance the operation? Their suspicions were confirmed in 1973, when De Lorean began canvassing GM dealers about their enthusiasm for a car built by the man who had helped make a lot of them very rich, and GM promptly jerked the benefits.

Though in 1973 a new car company headed by John De Lorean was still myth and speculation, the idea of the corporate renegade taking on mighty General Motors was catnip to the media, and JZD loved acting the part. "If GM is playing the piano," he stated in an interview in 1976, "we want to find a place somewhere between the keys where there is room to succeed." The cars he wanted to build, he said, were the ones GM disdained because they didn't offer enough volume to produce meaningful profits.

The stated model for the De Lorean dream was BMW, a German manufacturer of highly regarded sports sedans which fit nicely between the keys of GM's piano, never having to meet any of the corporation's products head-on on the marketplace. What made BMW special—and able to withstand the price hikes which plagued German automakers in the late Seventies—was a line of cars that satisfied both the driver/enthusiast and the owner looking for an automotive status symbol. Moreover, BMW's are expensive, and like Mercedes, Porsche (and to a lesser extent Cadillac) buyers in the upper income brackets can still afford to buy or lease a new car even when times are tough. In 1981, when Detroit was reporting record losses, Mercedes had its biggest U.S. year ever.

In 1971 De Lorean led Chevy, but moved to GM Corporate in 1972 and left six months later, although rumors persist that President Ed Cole (below) asked him to go. (General Motors)

A Six-Series BMW coupe, precisely the market segment John De Lorean felt there was room to fit into. (BMW)

The Bricklin SV-1 appeared in 1974 and had ceased production by the beginning of 1976 with fewer than 3,000 built. The Ford-powered gullwing coupe suffered from numerous design and construction problems.

Piano playing with the media is one thing, emulating BMW's climb from the bombed-out ruins of Munich to a place of pre-eminence in the world car market another. For De Lorean to turn his dream into reality was going to take an enormous amount of money—and the precedent for raising such automotive risk capital was, in a word—awful. Looking back at the De Lorean investment potential, one Wall Street expert commented in 1981, "When people asked my advice about investing in De Lorean's venture, I told them to put the money into wine, women and song. I figured they'd get the same return and have more fun." Prophetic words.

De Lorean Versus Bricklin

While John De Lorean was trying to get his new automobile company launched there was a tendency on the part of many skeptics to compare De Lorean's aims with those of Malcolm Bricklin. The latter had become a millionaire by the time he was 25 years old and at the age of 35 declared he would build a $3,000 "safety" sports car fitted with gullwing doors. You can see why one might be tempted to draw parallels.

There's no denying Malcolm Bricklin was a man who could get things done. In addition to amassing his wealth, he was also involved in the early years of importing Subaru automobiles to the U.S. Bricklin set a short timetable to get his SV-1 sports car into production. His initial backing came with $500,000 from the First Pennsylvania Banking & Trust Co. and by autumn, 1972, there was a Bricklin Vehicle Corporation building in Livonia, Michigan with a small staff of design and engineering people. Then came negotiations with the Canadian government to have the Bricklin factory established in job-poor New Brunswick, a deal that was made in June, 1973, and included investment in the company through Bricklin Canada Ltd. that was initially set at some $9 million

with another $2.8 million in loans.

There were problems of several natures that followed the Bricklin. Some were political, Premier Hatfield, who was backing Bricklin's project, having to fight John Turnbull of the Opposition Party over the money invested with the automaker. It was also turning out that building a new automobile from scratch was more expensive and time consuming than Malcolm Bricklin had anticipated. Another problem was getting the necessary professional talent to move to New Brunswick. Naturally there was, and always would be the problem of money.

The Bricklin SV-1 was introduced in New York City in summer, 1974, with the promise of 1,000 cars per month off the assembly line by autumn. There was even a press junket in August to show off the first production car, yet by Thanksgiving only a few hundred Bricklins had been built, some missing pieces that were on back order. Even completed Bricklins were plagued with problems, some small, others quite critical. The gullwing doors were one. I remember driving through a rainstorm in a Bricklin only to arrive at a dinner to discover the sport coat I had left in the area behind the seats was completely soaked with water.

A total of 780 Bricklins were built in 1974 using American Motors 360-cubic-inch V-8s, most with Chrysler 3-speed automatic transmissions and a few with a 4-speed manual gearbox. The following year the company changed to the Ford 351-cubic-inch V-8 and automatic gearbox only. The result was 2,100 cars produced, but at an ever-growing political and financial cost to New Brunswick and to Hatfield, who had managed to weather his last election. As losses mounted, Bricklin went looking for money in both the U.S. and Canada, but any possible sources had dried up. The price of the SV-1 had climbed from $7,490 at introduction to $9,980, thanks in part to the switch to Ford engines, and yet quality was still marginal. In

*It would be easy—but inaccurate—
to compare Malcolm Bricklin's
attempt at car manufacturing with
that of John De Lorean. In personality, approach and experience the
two are world's apart, and similarly,
the cars are not comparable.*
(Road & Track)

November, 1975, foreclosure was begun against Bricklin. The few remaining cars were moved through the assembly line, the last 17 being the only 1976 Bricklins built. The last 300 cars and the company's assets were bought by Consolidated International of Columbus, Ohio (the same firm that "bought" 1,200 De Loreans in late spring, 1982, to help DMC out of one financial crisis and, later would buy the De Loreans that remained when DMC declared bankruptcy).

More Than Blue Jeans

What then of the comparison between Malcolm Bricklin and John Z. De Lorean? They certainly shared the same objective: a gullwing sports car with the original intentions of becoming a safety car. And both men have the sort of impassioned strength needed to get such a monumental project under way. They had their dream and could find their investors. There was, however, a critical difference between Bricklin and De Lorean and it was much more than Mal Bricklin's blue jeans and cowboy hat versus John De Lorean's pinstripe suit and absolutely correct hair-cut. Bricklin made much of his money outside the automobile industry and then tried to buy his way in, once commenting to Ron Wakefield of *Road & Track,* "I run this the way I see it. No market research. I know the guy we're building this car for. He's the guy who

wants a beautiful car but doesn't know a f----n' thing about cars." Adding later, "That's me."

De Lorean grew up wanting to be a part of the auto industry. He has a degree in automotive engineering, a master's in business administration and years of experience working his way up through the largest automotive corporation in the world. Bricklin seemed to think that merely getting his car into production was enough . . . no need to be concerned that the first 400 SV-1's were shipped minus such necessary pieces as their sound insulation . . . production actually preceded final engineering. De Lorean tried to hold on to his automobile until it was right, even if there are those who now charge he outdated his automobile before it was in production.

And yet the Bricklin and De Lorean automobiles did come to the same end. Does it mean that no one can make such a company succeed? Probably not. In keeping with the profile of the entrepreneur presented in Chapter 1, the failure of both firms suggests that the temperament needed to get an automobile company started is different than the motivations necessary in the men who can turn such a new company into a continuing success. Henry M. Leland started *both* the Cadillac and Lincoln Motor Companys, but it was Alfred P. Sloan at General Motors and Henry Ford II at Ford that made the two cars successful. Leland is now only a footnote in automotive history. In fact, no one has managed to take a U.S. automotive company from start-up to success since Walter P. Chrysler bought Maxwell-Chalmers in 1923 as the first building block to his empire. Henry Kaiser and Joseph Frazer started manufacturing their automobiles in an ex-bomber factory in Willow Run, Michigan in 1946, only to fail a decade and $100 million later. Preston Tucker was also going to advance the state of the art with the Tucker Torpedo. His company came and went in four years. The lawsuits between the Securities and

Exchange Commission and Tucker (who was finally vindicated) went on for even longer.

Just as discouraging to consider are the famous automotive marques which have died since World War II. Packard, one-time standard of luxury cars in America, disappeared in 1958 after two years as an ugly redo of the Studebaker. Packard's demise was probably not lost on John De Lorean, because he was the company's Director of Research before leaving there. In 1966 Studebaker, begun in 1852 as a carriage manufacturer, went out of existence. It's significant to note that the one part of Studebaker that did not die, and continues basically unchanged to this day, is the Avanti, a high-priced and to some minds sporty and distinctive luxury automobile. Just as significant, perhaps, is that unlike the De Lorean, which offered one exterior finish and a minimum of interior colors,

Avanti provides its customers a huge choice of exterior colors and interior seat and door panel coverings and carpeting. However, this small South Bend, Indiana company lives with a down-to-earth overhead that would probably be considered tacky in a company operated by John De Lorean.

Doom And Gloom

If this history isn't enough doom and gloom, remember that the De Lorean Motor Company was started just after the 1973 Arab Oil Boycott. Gasoline prices had really taken off and with that and other rapidly increasing energy costs came inflation . . . at a time when double-digit inflation had previously been a problem only other nations suffered. Buyers were upset Detroit wasn't building small economical cars, and yet would abandon the fuel mizers and go back

The Avanti, introduced by Studebaker in 1962, still remains in production. Its fiberglass body was styled by Raymond Loewy. (Studebaker)

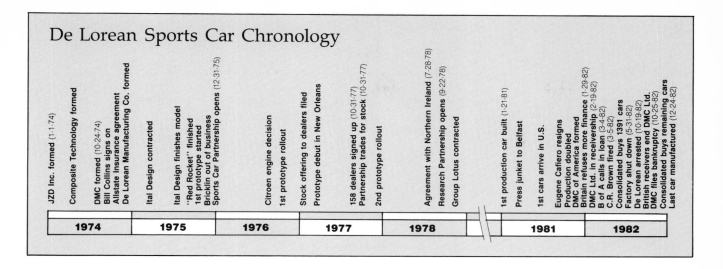

to big automobiles the moment the price and availability of gasoline improved. Detroit executives were on the verge of making some of the worst mistakes in the industry's history and there was, in general, a great deal of mistrust flowing between consumers, automakers and, hovering in the wings, the federal government.

Timing is the essence of humor, and to some observers it was laughable to try to begin a new automobile company in 1975. And just how much money would De Lorean need? Inflation, among other things, made De Lorean's money goals into moving targets. One of the original estimates was for $77 million—$7 million to design and build prototype automobiles, find a plant site and establish a dealer's system; $20 million to ready the car for production, design the factory and begin market development; $35 million to build the plant and fabricate all the tooling needed; and $15 million as working capital to bring the sports car to the start of production.

Originally it was thought the $77 million would be raised in five basic sources: John De Lorean himself, a limited partnership of individual investors, stock bought by dealers, a public stock offering and, with the confidence established after achieving the first four steps, the remainder ($15 million) could be arranged in loans from banks. That's not quite the way it worked out.

Our scenario opens on January 1, 1974, with the formation of the John Z. De Lorean Corporation. JZDC didn't build cars, but offered advice on the subjects of general business management, marketing and production. The next building block was a subsidiary company JZDC began in April, 1975. Named Composite Technology Corporation, it was meant to be the arm of the corporation that would develop applications and production techniques for the Elastic Reservoir Molding (ERM) process for which De Lorean had

taken a license from Royal Dutch Shell in the Netherlands. This method of sandwiching foam between sheets of fiberglass was planned to be used in the De Lorean car. CTC was the first of a line of companies and partnerships set up to develop, build and sell De Loreans.

On October 24, 1975, the De Lorean Motor Company (DMC) was officially established and shortly thereafter JZDC—which wholly owned the new DMC—changed its name to De Lorean Manufacturing Company. From here on things can get a bit confusing, with the development of the various investor partnerships, so we've broken it down on a reference chart . . . like the list of names and relationships one needs when reading many Russian novels.

Although the De Lorean car began its life, so to speak, in Bloomfield Hills, Michigan, most of the action after the completion of the first two prototypes took place in New York; Irvine and Santa Ana, California; and Bridgewater, New Jersey. In the latter two locations were the Quality Assurance Centers, in which the new cars were gone over before being shipped to dealers. These QAC's were intended as temporary until the desired quality could be achieved off the production line. The Irvine building was headquarters for C. R. "Dick" Brown during his time with DMC, and was subsequently occupied by Bruce McWilliams and then Don Lander. These facilities paled in comparison with DMC's New York offices. Located at prestigious 280 Park Ave., the company rented half of the 43rd floor and half of the 35th. The furnishings were consistent with the address, and made for a splendid environment for those working there. But the offices also became a symbol of extravagance that angered the British, who were by then footing the bill for the sports car project, and were a matter of concern to DMC executives, who knew it was just too rich for such a young company.

2

Developing The Prototype

I T WASN'T EASY for Bill Collins to pack it in at General Motors and go to work with John De Lorean. After 20 years with GM, Collins had risen to the job of Assistant Chief Engineer at Pontiac, likely to succeed his boss, Steve Malone, when he retired. The seal of approval for Collins' future had been given by GM when he was put in charge of the engineering redesign of its B-cars. These were the largest of the corporation's models and the first to be "downsized," with introduction targeted for the 1977 model year. There had been a great deal of anguish about all this at GM, because any change beyond longer, lower and wider simply hadn't been part of their serious corporate plan. Then the first Arab Oil Boycott in 1973 pinned Detroit up against the wall and they had to start producing smaller automobiles. Shrinking the high-profit B-car was a radical philosophical challenge for such a traditional car company.

So, when Bill Collins was made Chief Engineer of the B-cars it was GM's way of saying he was headed for a big future in the corporation. Those of us in the press were delighted. There are enough traditionalist, unimaginative engineers in Detroit that the automotive writers can quickly pick out the engineers who don't have mere slide rules for brains. John De Lorean had been another one. Company men, but men who can appreciate that GM doesn't always get everything right and that automobiles should be referred to and appreciated as automobiles and not "units," which is the term often used by those in the sales and marketing departments.

There's another entire book about that latter sentence and what it cost Detroit in sales and profits during the late Seventies and early Eighties, but it also points out why many automotive writers were both surprised and yet understanding when Bill Collins resigned from GM and started with John De Lorean in October, 1974. The pair had worked together closely at Pontiac during De Lorean's expansive years at that division, and Collins was one of the men responsible for the original GTO and Trans-Am projects in that division, being key in developing the last of the great Pontiacs before that division began its general decline in the mid-Seventies. So the combination of De Lorean and Collins seemed a natural. The Pontiac engineer would lose a great deal by leaving GM, but he'd also be working with someone he knew and understood, unencumbered by a big corporation's paperwork, brow-beating and dictates. Collins knew the development of the De Lorean DMC-12 would be the greatest thing in his life.

For Collins' first night in a De Lorean company car—Oct. 1, 1974—he drove home in a 1936 Ford. This wasn't because of corporate money problems, but because the Ford had a stainless steel body, and this was the material De Lorean planned for the body of his sports car. The Ford had been built in the Thirties by Allegheny Ludlum, which was trying to promote the many virtues of stainless steel. And Collins, who had owned a rusting 1936 Ford as a teenager, was impressed. That same autumn he also drove a 1967 Lincoln 4-door convertible skinned in the same material. "I was impressed with it," Collins comments. "I'd park it under my maple trees, and if you did that in the fall with a white car you'd end up with brown spots all over it, but the stainless steel washed off very well. I thought it was kind of a keen idea . . . ."

De Lorean's Design Parameters

That example points up the manner in which Collins would work with the parameters set by De Lorean for his sports car. There simply weren't any basic problems between the two on the matter, and Collins set out to design what De Lorean wanted, i.e. a gentleman's sports car with dramatic styling, an

Bill Collins explaining the ERM "sandwich." (Lamm)

engine in back, stainless steel bodywork, gullwing doors, and good performance. The car was also to be based on the philosophy that it was a responsibly designed and built automobile offering a high degree of safety and good fuel economy, and would not be the sort of car you'd have to dispose of in a few years. And since De Lorean is 6 ft. 4 in. tall and Collins measures in at 6 ft. 3 in., it was to accommodate tall men.

Much of the philosophy of the De Lorean Safety Vehicle (DSV-1), as it was known then, was described by a November, 1974, agreement between De Lorean and the Allstate Insurance Company to create what became the De Lorean Sports Car . . . and which provided $500,000 of seed money for the project. Allstate wanted a so-called safety vehicle to demonstrate that the qualities an insurance company finds most desirable in an automobile—still-better occupant protection, economical service and repair, improved damageability protection in low- and high-speed accident, advanced anti-theft methods, and competent accident avoidance—needn't come in a big, fat and ugly automobile.

AMF's answer to a government contract for a safety car.

This was happening, it should be remembered, on the heels of a safety movement within the U.S. government (with endorsement by much of the insurance industry) that began with Public Law 89-563, otherwise known as the "National Traffic and Motor Vehicle Safety Act of 1966." Millions of dollars had been spent on proposed means of saving more of the lives and money lost in auto accidents. Among other things, several huge and heavy experimental safety cars were built under government contract by such companies as AMF and Fairchild Hiller to prove that

23

Part of the Federal government's safety car program involved "crash offs" between several of the cars. Here the AMF-designed "Experimental Safety Vehicle" (right) meets Toyota's entry. Originally, the De Lorean (with financing from Allstate Insurance) was to have many of the safety capabilities of government cars, but in a smaller, lighter and certainly more attractive package.

drivers could be saved from themselves and each other. The automotive press, Detroit and others involved closely with automobiles and how to design, build and drive them did not consider the general governmental mood to be exactly enlightened.

The Allstate-De Lorean Safety Vehicles

De Lorean's and Allstate's safety vehicle proposal came two years and one Arab oil crisis after the big crash-off and was a much more reasonable approach. The contracted pair of vehicles to be built were to meet or exceed all federal vehicle safety standards, including a passive front occupant restraint system (meaning the driver and passenger need make no effort to protect themselves, such as hooking up a seatbelt) with the capacity to meet the governmental injury criteria in crashes into a solid barrier at speeds up to 40 mph and, perhaps, 50 mph. The car was to suffer no front- or rear-end damage in a 10-mph slam into a barrier. All engine anti-pollution laws were to be met. Interior designs were to cause minimum driver fatigue. The car should be easily repairable. There were to be no protruding parts on the exterior that might injure pedestrians hit by the car. Driver and passenger should be easy to rescue after any one of several types of accidents (which made the gullwing doors an interesting choice). Anti-theft equipment was to be used. Driver control of the car was to be considered for better handling and braking, including an anti-skid braking system. The car shouldn't weigh more than 2,500 pounds minus passengers and luggage, and get no less than 25 mpg at a sustained 50 mph.

Dimensions for the Allstate-De Lorean were to include a 90-inch wheelbase, and overall length, height and width of not less than, respectively, 160, 40 and 70 inches. Most important of all, perhaps, is that the Allstate-De Lorean should be attractive enough to be sold to the general public and then at a price of around

$7,000 in 1974 dollars with a production schedule of 50,000 cars per year.

With a starting date of November 1, 1974, there were numerous completion dates for various parts of the program, but prototypes were to be ready for drive and crash testing by December 1, 1975. When the project was completed, De Lorean would have the rights to manufacture and sell the sports car. All of these dates shortly became academic when Allstate lost interest in the project, tipped its safety hat and said goodby, leaving behind its half-million dollar investment in the good hands of John Zachary De Lorean.

Finding The "H" Point

How do you start with a blank sheet of paper and design a sports car? Bill Collins remembers those first months: "Basically I just sat down and went through all my experience with the 1977 B-car program and the old Pontiac XP833 [a middle-Sixties 2-seater sports car project that was to be Pontiac's version of the Corvette—Ed.] and built up the things we needed—ground clearance, what the ride travel has to be, then adding the driver with his "h" point [a point that indicates where the driver's hip is in relation to other measurements in the car—Ed.] as close to the ground as you can, crank in how far you want him to be able to move to the rear, the back angle and the headroom you want and now you know how high the car is to be."

One of the basic requirements was, of course, the gullwing doors, which Collins liked. "The only guy who gave me a hassle on that was Karl Ludvigsen (one of America's most highly respected automotive journalists, for a short time a De Lorean consultant and now a Vice President with Ford of Europe). Karl said, 'If you look around you'll notice all the doors in the world are hinged vertically and there must be a very good reason for that.' The gullwing doors, to me, were a good solution. They do a couple of things for you: One, they let you get into a car that's very low and, two, they swing out very little. Try to get into a Lotus Esprit and you've got a real problem in those aspects.''

300SL—The "Original" Gullwing

Inevitably, the gullwing doors of the De Lorean bring memories of the "original" gullwing car, the Mercedes-Benz 300SL. Yet it's possible to argue that the only thing the two cars have in common are those doors. And the flip-up doors were used on the two cars for different reasons.

Mercedes' 300SL—the "SL" meaning Sport-Light—was originally a racing car, first introduced in March, 1952, and subsequently raced successfully everywhere from the Mille Miglia in Italy, to Le Mans in France to the Mexican Road Race, the latter won in 1952 by Karl Kling in one of the Mercedes coupes. These competition cars led to the most commonly known 300SL, the production version which debuted in February, 1954, at New York's International Motor Sports Show.

All non-convertible 300SLs had gullwing doors, though in the early race cars they were only flip-up windows that took a small section of roof with them when they swung up. The purpose of both the small racing gullwings and the "full-size" doors on the production car was the same. Mercedes engineers, led by the legendary Rudolf Uhlenhaut, designed the 300SL's around a space frame. This foundation for the car is a series of tubes welded together to form the inner structure, into which the drivetrain and suspensions are bolted and around which the body is added. To get maximum strength, the 300SL's frame design needed to be quite high on the sides where the doors would normally be fitted. The racing regulations to which those early 300SL's were built didn't say how the doors must be hinged, so Mercedes used the gull-

Two Mercedes-Benz legends: Engineer Rudolf Uhlenhaut in the original 300SL Coupe. By using the flip-up "doors," Mercedes was able to design the car's frame to be waist high and more rigid than with normal doors. (Kurt Wörner)

wings. With development, the height of the frame sides could be lowered as they subsequently were, until the production 300SL had a very reasonable height to the door opening, though the width of the opening still presented a problem to ladies wearing tight skirts.

So the production 300SL began life with gullwing doors, and a racing heritage. Its drivetrain was based on a production engine, like the De Lorean, but the inline-6 was Mercedes' own. Though it only produced 150 horsepower in the 300S model in which it was used when the 300SL project was started, by the time it was in the production 300SL the engine had 215 hp. With a curb weight of 2,900 lb, the Mercedes carried about 13.5 lb for every horsepower it produced, while the

2,750-lb, 130-horsepower De Lorean has 21.1 lb-per-horsepower, which means dramatically better performance for the 300SL. *Road & Track* once managed a 0-60 mph time for the 300SL of 8.2 seconds, while the De Lorean they tested needed 10.5 seconds . . . as crucial a difference in the enthusiast's mind as it is on the road.

Right from the start the 300SL was a hit. Mercedes never built more of their sports cars than was necessary—an even 1,400 gullwing coupes and total of 3,258 when you add in the roadsters—about the same number of cars De Lorean sold in 1981.

Some Daimler-Benz executives weren't certain they should be building the car at all, preferring to stick with the much more profitable sedans and trucks. In fact, at the original asking price of $6,820—probably not far off the De Lorean's 1981 asking price when you factor in inflation—Mercedes was losing money on the 300SL, but profiting by the tremendous effect the car had on the company's image, both on the race track and at very fashionable country clubs. Today, a like-new 300SL gullwing could draw as high as $100,000 on a combination of aura and engineering that allow you to admire the car's aggressive styling and then assure you that as soon as you pull down that door, start the engine and drive off you are in a rock-solid, race-bred automobile that demands and delivers a great deal. 300SL's are *still* bolstering the Mercedes-Benz image.

For their series of C111 sports cars, which did everything from showcase the Wankel rotary engine to set world speed and endurance records, Mercedes retained gullwing doors. There may have been some nostalgia involved in once again using these doors, but they were also part of an engineering solution. Mercedes wanted to keep the cars' weight balanced, so the fuel tanks were placed in the door sills, once again making them quite high and requiring gullwing

doors. Would Mercedes again use gullwings in a production sports car? It seems unlikely (and unfortunate), because Daimler-Benz is now even larger, more profitable and conservative than in 1954.

Serious Engineering Versus Serious Marketing

While the 300SL had gullwing doors for serious engineering reasons, the De Lorean had them as much for serious marketing reasons as for engineering. It's possible to argue that these days one is as crucial as the other. Because the car had gullwing doors, De Lorean engineers were able to take advantage of the high door sills for more structure and crash protection, but these were icing on the cake. It was the door's image that counted initially.

Another important difference between the 300SL and De Lorean gullwing doors stems from what the, automakers', required of them. All the Mercedes' had to be was a door. Period. It had to open and close, but Mercedes never even attempted to give it a roll-down window. If you want fresh air in a gullwing 300SL you snap open a vent window or completely remove the main one. As a result of this simplicity and a higher sill height than the De Lorean, the 300SL gullwing door is thin and light. The De Lorean door had to be longer, contain the usual latching system, air conditioning ducting, a small power window, little lights in the door edges and electrically-operated door locks, all of which add a great deal to the door's complexity and weight.

In hindsight it is now possible to argue that the missing sales ingredient in the De Lorean is the background image and engineering aura you can find in the racing exploits of 300SL's, Porsche, Maseratis, Aston Martins, Corvettes, Ferraris and other such successful automobiles. Those competition ventures not only add to the automobile in real engineering terms, but can provide a heritage and a psychological boost

Giorgetto Giugiaro's original design for the Lotus Esprit. Called project M70, the car was introduced at the 1972 Turin Show. It was one of the cars that marked the designer's move from the more sweeping lines of the Sixties to the sharper edges of the Seventies. The shape was subtly changed for production. (Ital Design)

to get their companies over rough times, drawing in at least a few customers who will buy on the basis of past performance alone. Lamborghini, another company that builds serious grand touring cars but never raced seriously, continues to tumble insecurely from receivership to receivership.

An automotive heritage is the one thing the De Lorean never had time to develop. While the history of cars such as the 300SL, many Ferraris, Maseratis and such will be told and retold in the pages of magazines such as *Road & Track, Car and Driver,* and *Motor Trend,* the De Lorean will be remembered as much by *Forbes* and *Fortune* as by the automotive magazines.

There are numerous other differences between the De Lorean and the 300SL, but perhaps the most crucial is simply this: The 300SL was both a research and development tool and an image builder for Mercedes-Benz, the gullwing De Lorean was its company's only product. Mercedes could afford to lose a little money on each car, while De Lorean spent his company into a position where it couldn't lose an unnecessary penny on any of its products.

Something To See And Touch

With the fundamental dimensions of the De Lorean worked out, Bill Collins now went to a company in Detroit known as Pioneer Engineering, which took the numbers and translated them into a basic seating package. The numbers and sketches became something they could see and touch when it was then made into a seating buck, and as Collins explains, ". . . that defined the cross section, because we knew we were going to have high sills and we knew we were going to have a very high center tunnel, because originally that was where the fuel tank was to be." The De Lorean was begun.

Next was the problem of just who would produce

the dramatic styling De Lorean knew his sports car would need. In November, 1974, De Lorean and Collins went to Europe and the Turin Auto Show to make the rounds of the major automobile coachbuilders to sound them out on the project. Turin, Italy, is the world's center of automotive styling and while there De Lorean and Collins visited four of the world's most famous automobile design firms: Bertone, Pininfarina, Michelotti and Ital Design. At Ital Design they met with the company's owner and chief designer, Giorgetto Giugiaro. Though only 36 at the time, Giugiaro was already considered perhaps the most brilliant single car designer in Italy, if not the world. Despite his age, the list of automobiles penned by Giugiaro, first when he worked with Bertone, then Ghia and finally for his own firm, Ital Design, is staggering.

While with Bertone, Giugiaro had designed such cars as the ASA 1000, Iso Rivolta, Alfa Romeo Guilia Sprint GT, Iso Grifo and Fiat Dino Coupe. At Ghia he is credited with, among others, the Isuzu 117 Coupe, DeTomaso Mangusta, Maserati Ghibli and the Ghia 450 SS. At the time De Lorean and Collins visited him, Giugiaro had already designed for his own company—and these are only the production automobiles, not the one-off show cars—the Maserati Bora and Merak; Alfa Romeo's Alfasud and Alfetta GT; Suzuki Fronte; Lotus Esprit; Volkswagen Dasher, Rabbit and Scirocco; and the Hyundai Pony.

De Lorean and Collins were so impressed they drew up a basic contract with Giugiaro. In February, 1975, the designer went to Detroit, where a more comprehensive interior buck had been built by a company called Design Caucus. This layout more completely defined the inside of the De Lorean DSV-12, as it was now known. After more discussion Giugiaro left for Italy and a month later a formal contract between Ital Design and De Lorean was signed.

Giugiaro's Styling Guidelines

As basic guidelines, Giugiaro was given a set of styling parameters which included five overall requirements: that it have lasting appeal, that it be practical and functional, that it meet all U.S. safety standards, that the drag coefficient be around 0.33 and, finally, that the car could be mass-produced, i.e. not a one shot. Then there was a more specific list of things the designer had to follow, including one-piece soft elastomer bumpers that fit flush with the body surface and that had an 8-inch stroke to allow compression in an accident. Exposed rectangular headlights were requested, because of the mechanical complexity of pop-up lights. The gullwing doors were part of that list and it was requested that they be thin and lightweight. There was to be protection from minor dents and scrapes for 360 degrees around the body at its widest point, which the designer could accomplish with soft elastomer plastic, and the door sill was high for added crash protection. A maximum windshield angle of 60 degrees was allowed, there could be no center windshield pillar and the radio antenna was to be in the front glass. A narrow center support for the gullwing doors was required to limit the amount they would have to swing outward and a roll bar was required as part of the partition between the passenger and engine compartments. There was to be a 100-square-inch opening in the rear end panel as a radiator air exit and that space could be either above, below or on both sides of the bumper. The De Lorean would also need a 98-square-inch radiator entrance that would flow about 1300 cubic feet of air each minute at 55 mph.

There was also a list of dimensions passed on to Ital Design that were fundamental to the De Lorean design. This is a matter of stacking design parameters, one atop the other, to develop such specifications as overall length, height and width. For height DMC decided they wanted 2.0 inches of ground clearance when the car was pressed downward on its suspension as far as the suspension would allow. To this they added ride travel—3.1 inches jounce in front and 3.6 inches at the back. There needed to be 1.75 inches from the lowest part of the seat when it was fully compressed to the bottom of the seat pan and then another .75 inch from there to the bottom of the underbody. They added 37.5 inches of headroom (". . . we wanted to be better than the Corvette and equal to a Firebird . . ."), to reach an overall height of 46.0 inches. Legroom was pegged at 43.7 inches, again better than the Corvette.

Other areas of the design package were dependent on the size of the elements they were to contain. The volume of the Pirelli P7 tires and the amount of wheel travel they required determined the "tire envelopes" within which they would move. The size of the proposed Citroën drivetrain, and the volume of luggage space in front, when added to the interior package, were figured to give an overall length. An overall width had to consider not just the passenger space, but also the room needed for the engine, transmission and driveshafts . . . and on and on to an automobile package size around which Giugiaro would have to sculpt the lines of the De Lorean.

Within a month the designer had sketches of six possible De Loreans ready*and De Lorean and Collins traveled to Turin and picked their favorite for more detail work. Giugiaro was back at the drawing board and about every three weeks Collins was back in Turin to see how things were progressing. The engineer was very impressed with the designer and said they never really had any arguments about the car. Collins explains, "The difference between working with a man like Giugiaro, who you have hired to do a job, and GM Design, which is the corporation's styling group,

See Color Salon #1, page 57

is totally different. Giugiaro would ask me what we wanted, what he had to do, and he never violated any of those requests.''

Initial Engine Evaluation

While Giugiaro was at the drawing board, Collins was busy in the States evaluating various engines that could be used in the sports car. De Lorean had been interested by the prospect of a Wankel rotary engine, the type that was built in 2- and 4-rotor form to go into two Corvettes that were designed when De Lorean was at Chevrolet. De Lorean had tried to buy the 2-rotor Corvette from GM, and there was a set of

engineering drawings for the car at DMC, but he'd been turned down in his bid for the lovely design. In hindsight this was really very unfortunate. Remember that GM had spent millions of dollars on the Wankel engine program before the powerplant took its lumps in the oil boycott and was dropped by the corporation. And yet the advantages of that engine in terms of the amount of power it produces for its size are impressive. There were also those who believed that the engine's durability and fuel economy problems were solvable and De Lorean was one (as was Kenichi Yamamoto at Mazda, the unassuming, brilliant engineer who became the Wankel's savior).

When General Motors Design did the styling of Chevrolet's four-rotor Corvette in the early Seventies, gullwing doors were used. These doors had a difference because they were hinged in the middle and stuck out less than "conventional" gullwings. (Chevrolet)

The first De Lorean prototype began as a Fiat X 1/9 that was, to say the least, modified. Shoehorned in to replace the Fiat 4-cylinder was a Ford V-6. The gearbox was a 5-speed Borg-Warner joined to the 2.8-liter V-6 by a chain drive. Early Pirelli P7 tires were used at the rear. The transmission innards ended up scattered all over an interstate highway near Detroit. (Bill Collins)

In 1974, however, there weren't many sources from which to buy such an engine. One potential Wankel source was in France, where Citroen and NSU had been working jointly in a company called Comotor to develop a Wankel automobile engine (NSU had already produced one Wankel model, the Ro80). Code numbered the 624, the Comotor engine was claimed to weigh 223 pounds and develop 107 horsepower at 6600 rpm and 101 foot-pounds of torque at 3000 rpm.

However, the Comotor project never happened. Collins visited their office while heading home from Turin in 1974. "I stopped and saw a guy at Comotor in Paris, but he had a tiny out-of-the-way office and it was obvious from talking to him they weren't going to be building Wankels much longer." Besides, the price tag was $900 per engine.

This desire to use a Wankel also had De Lorean talking with Mazda's parent company, Toyo Kogyo, through U.S. Wankel licensee Curtis-Wright, but things never got too serious. The engine considered was TKK's 2-rotor 12B Wankel which produced 109 horsepower at 6300 rpm and 104 foot-pounds of torque at 4000 rpm.

After looking at a number of other possible engines—General Motors' 2.5-liter 4-cylinder was even noted in one proposal—Collins homed in on the Ford 119-horsepower, 2.8-liter German-built V-6 then being used in the Ford Mustang II and the Mercury Capri II. There was even speculation that the V-6 could be turbocharged in 2.6- or 2.8-liter form, which would have produced, respectively, 175 and 218 horsepower.

Pocobello's "Red Rocket"

At this point one of the other major characters in the development of the first De Lorean prototype enters the program. Mike Pocobello, a former Chevrolet engineer, had developed an excellent reputation while working on Jim Hall's famed Chaparral racing team. He now had his own Detroit-based independent engineering firm, Triad, which had previously done some work for John De Lorean on a motor home project for W.R. Grace Inc. So, it was natural that Collins would go there to continue development work on a De Lorean drivetrain, and out of it came the "Red Rocket."

The "Red Rocket" started life as a used Fiat X1/9 which Collins bought in mint condition from a Chrysler designer. (". . . the guy loved the car . . . the thing was just perfect. I didn't tell him what I was going to do with it.") Pocobello shoehorned in not just the V-6, but a homebuilt gearbox and rear suspension with fat Pirelli P7s tires. The X1/9 was no longer perfect.

The Ford V-6 was placed sideways in the Fiat's engine bay behind the rear axle as a true rear-engine car. The engine was placed so the clutch was on the left as you looked into the engine compartment. On the end of the clutch was a Morse chain that ran the power forward to a Borg-Warner T-5 5-speed manual transmission that sat parallel to the V-6. At the end of the T-5 was a gearcase and a differential that then sent the power to the halfshafts. The plan was to have the Red Rocket ready by October 1, 1975.

In the meantime, Collins—and, on occasion, John De Lorean—was making regular trips to Ital Design to check on the progress of the car's styling. During one such trip, the pair went to Porsche to investigate the possibility of having the German firm do the engineering of the De Lorean. They wanted too much money and required too much time. On another journey, Collins also stopped to discuss the engineering with Matra. This fishing about was De Lorean's idea, and Collins was not certain about hiring a firm to engineer your automobile when they build a similar car in the same price class.

While in Turin with Giugiaro, Collins and De Lorean were presented with a basic automobile

Giugiaro took Polaroid photos of the original styling mock-up and, using a felt-tip pen, sketched several possible design variations for John De Lorean and Bill Collins. Number 2 is the basic configuration for the first protype. When the car's shape needed to be "tweaked" after the project went to Lotus, Giugiaro made changes so the De Lorean wound up looking like design Number 1. (Bill Collins Collection)

shape in the form of a full-size model with the initials "JZD" in its front grille. The Italian still had a variety of designs for the upper half of the car's body. Giugiaro would sketch some design variations by taking Polaroid photos or making copies of Polaroids of the car and then revise them with a felt-tip pen to show different greenhouse treatments. A dozen of these were done and any fan of Giugiaro's will see window themes that have graced other of the designer's creations. The greenhouse styling that made its way to production on the lovely Giugiaro-designed BMW M1 shows up in one suggestion. In the end it was the design marked number two that De Lorean and Collins approved. Ital Design began work on the final version of the styling mock-up made from "epo-wood" that was due to be shipped to De Lorean in Detroit on July 31, 1975.

Giugiaro Styling Rationale

Giugiaro comments about the De Lorean: "I aimed to give this car, my first one for the States, a classical and sports look, without leaving out the American "Grandeur" look. I obtained this solid and roomy look by the design of a really large bonnet completely flat and the flattened horizontal radiator grille. You must remember that I worked on a DMC scheme without knowing precisely the car's central engine and mechanics."

As for the gullwing doors, the designer adds, "They are exotic, because they distinguish the model from others in the 'grandturismo' series. Furthermore, they give the advantage of making it easier for passengers to get in and out, as in the case of obstacles next to the vehicle's side as in garages, narrow streets and parking. The gullwing doors also make it possible to increase the car's sill structure height under the door line, making it stronger. The window portion under the door cut line has been expressly requested

4

8

5

9

6

10

7

11

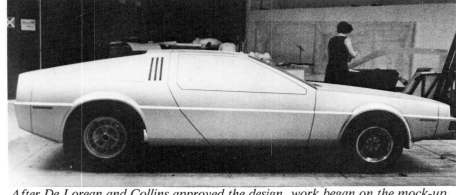

After De Lorean and Collins approved the design, work began on the mock-up.

Giugiaro working with a detail of the De Lorean epo-wood prototype (below). Collins was impressed with the Italian designer's reaction time, and also the manner in which he readily worked with DMC's requests. (Collins Collection)

The epo-wood styling mock-up being detailed before the final showing to DMC.

In America drawings would detail a car's final shape, but in Italy the mock-up provides the critical dimensions.

During a visit to Ital Design, John De Lorean discusses the design with Giugiaro. Notice the "JZD" initials on the front grille of the styling mock-up. De Lorean requested the deeper side windows (compared to the design that reached production) because it offered somewhat better side visibility for the driver. (Collins Collection)

by John De Lorean in order to allow more side visibility." As for the inside of the car, Giugiaro says, "John De Lorean asked for a really classical interior, without revolutionary novelties in the concept of the dashboard and the padding patterns."

Near the end of July, Collins finally made the trip to Ital Design to approve the final epo-wood styling model and the interior buck that was also called for in the contract. A pair of scale models for use in wind tunnel testing would be sent along later. When it finally arrived, the mock-up was sent to Design Caucus, the firm making the first set of pine die models from which

With the exterior styling mock-up, DMC also got a "buck" of the interior styling. Bill Collins is seen next to and sitting in the proposed interior. This design provided several passive safety features that fit the safety car image. (Collins Collection)

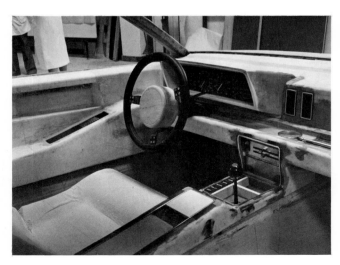

Among the design possibilities from Ital Design was this variety of suggested instrument panels for the De Lorean. An early feature of the car that never made it to production was a comprehensive master warning light system. (Collins Collection)

Milford Fabricating in Detroit would press the initial stainless steel body panels.

Scratch One Rocket

Eventually the mock-up and all the pieces were moved to Pocobello's Triad group, which was then working out of a building owned by a company called Kar Kraft. Automobile racing fans will remember this as the firm that built many of Ford's race cars in the years of that company's heavy competition involvement. One of the main people in that

Ital Design provided a pair of models to be used for wind tunnel testing. Bill Collins and Zora-Arkus Duntov took the models to Cal Tech's low-speed wind tunnel. They found the car needed a down-in-front attitude to prevent front-end lift. (Collins) At Design Caucus (right) the first set of pine die models were built, from which the stainless panels were then stamped. (Karl Ludvigsen)

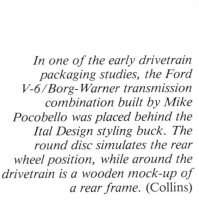

In one of the early drivetrain packaging studies, the Ford V-6/Borg-Warner transmission combination built by Mike Pocobello was placed behind the Ital Design styling buck. The round disc simulates the rear wheel position, while around the drivetrain is a wooden mock-up of a rear frame. (Collins)

venture, Chuck Mountain, was still at Kar Kraft, and would help Pocobello build the first car.

All this activity was taking place in the autumn of 1975—and right about then the Red Rocket was finished. . .but there were problems. As ingenious as the drivetrain design may have been with its readily available production parts, there was one fatal foible. The inertia of the Morse chain connecting the engine and gearbox, when added to the rotating inertia in the transmission, kept the latter rolling too long and too decisively. On each shift the gear synchronizers were strained and it was obvious they would never hold up over the long run. "The Red Rocket was kind of fun to drive," Pocobello recalls, "but then I scattered the driveline all over the ground one morning going to the airport. . .blew the transfer case into a million pieces all over I-94." They redesigned the transfer case and even made the necessary pattern changes, but shortly thereafter it was decided to drop the idea of using the Ford V-6. The little fat-tired Fiat was scrapped.

The Ford V-6 was abandoned in favor of the complete drivetrain from a French Citroën CX 2000. This engine and gearbox had been designed and proved in production as one unit. One other valuable lesson learned from the Fiat was that the experimental Pirelli P7 tires fitted in the back were very impressive, and they now became a part of the De Lorean chassis package. As Pocobello describes it, "We didn't do anything but screw on the new tires (the P7's on the X1/9) and it was a brand new car. Just unbelievable."

Looking For Mr. Goodbar

As Collins and Triad began work on the first prototype, John De Lorean started looking for the funds needed to build his automobile. First on the list of outside sources for De Lorean was the formation of the De Lorean Sports Car Partnership, a program that was put together by Hamilton Gregg of Gregg

A Citroën CX drivetrain with its 4-cylinder engine and 4-speed gearbox was used in the first prototype. It was a compact, proven combination that allowed the car to be mid-engine, but the 4-cylinder lacked power. (Collins)

and Wardell in New York City. This was begun at the same time as the De Lorean Motor Company in October, 1975, and on December 31, 1975, all the rights to the sports car—the company's only real automotive asset—were transferred to the Partnership. DMC as general partners had a 49.9 percent interest, a company officer held 0.1 percent and the limited partners would have a total of 50 percent interest. The money that would be raised by this offering was to be used to design, build, and develop three prototypes. There would be money for crash testing, work on developing the organization and a chance to begin developing the dealer network. The ante was $100,000

This is the prospectus describing the De Lorean Sports Car Partnership, which was successful, and raised $3.5 million. The interests of the Partnership were subsequently exchanged for stock in DMC.

for each investor and was considered in Securities and Exchange Commission terms—and, to many, in real terms—as a high risk.

It was, however, a relative risk to investors in that tax bracket. Because the money was meant for research and development work, there was an excellent chance the investor could count on a portion of his $100,000 being returned after taxes, the precise amount depending on his tax bracket. Beyond that there were almost endless possibilities for the investor predicated on scenarios that ranged from corporate disaster to stunning success, none of which would hurt them financially if they were in a position to get in in the first place. The offering of the Partnership was successful, bringing in the proposed $3.5 million. (On October 31, 1977, DMC picked up the option to dissolve the Partnership by trading their interest for 99,995 shares of DMC's $8 cumulative convertible preferred stock. So each of the partners—10 of whom were automobile dealers—now had 2,857 shares of DMC stock, just as advertised in the original offering. If the company had grown to be successful, those 35 high-tax bracket investors would have been still wealthier.)

Hold The ERM Sandwich

In late October, 1975, work finally began on the first prototype, Bill Collins interpreting John De Lorean's thoughts on what the car should be to Mike Pocobello and Chuck Mountain, who then turned Collins' ideas into hardware. There were a few production pieces that would go into the car in addition to the Citroën drivetrain, such as a Ford Pinto steering knuckle and upper control arm in the front suspension and a Ford rack and pinion steering, but much of the rest was fabricated by Kar Kraft.

At the heart of this new car would be ERM. This was the Elastic Reservoir Molding process for which

De Lorean had bought a number of licenses and formed Composite Technology Corporation. Perhaps best described as a plastic sandwich, it involves two 1/2-inch thick sheets of open-cell urethane foam with resin between them. This becomes the center of the sandwich between upper and lower layers of fiberglass, and when all this is put in a die or press and squeezed down to about 4 mm thickness it produces a panel with excellent strength for its weight and good energy absorbance. Though relatively low pressures—in the 50-150 psi range—are used, the resin is squeezed through the foam and the fiberglass mat, leaving a very dense foam core. In thicker sections ERM can be formed around high-density urethane foam, the latter adding extra strength without a great deal of weight. For the De Lorean sports car it would even be possible to combine a stainless steel outer panel with a ERM bonded inside to add rigidity. One important anticipated advantage of the ERM was that it required only resin dies rather than expensive metal dies.

ERM, however, would have to wait. Though it was meant to be the technical pearl in the De Lorean, there were a number of questions about ERM that had to be resolved, and so the first prototype's inner body would be done in standard hand lay-up fiberglass. This 'glass was meant for the car's inner structure, in which an upper and lower half would be joined like the two pieces of a model airplane's fuselage. A roof structure made of steel and called a "spider" would be mounted atop this inner body to take the added weight of the gullwing doors. A steel front subframe would carry the front suspension, while a larger rear steel subframe-cum-engine bay would contain both the Citroën drivetrain and the rear suspension. These subframes would then bolt up into the inner body. Covering all this would be Giugiaro's shape executed in stainless steel.

It was up to Triad to design and Kar Kraft to build

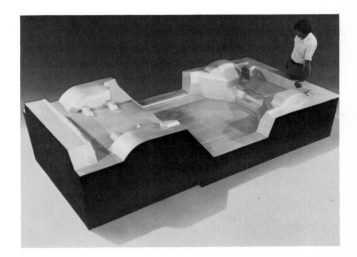

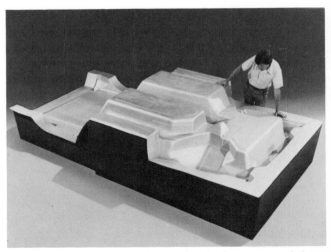

This is the tooling created to make the inner core of the first De Lorean prototype. Designed by Triad and made by Kar Kraft, the tooling was used to make the upper and lower halves of the underbody. (Collins Collection)

The first De Lorean prototype was designed by Triad on Bill Collins' concepts and built by Kar Kraft. While some production parts were used, such as the Citroën drivetrain, many of the pieces were built from scratch in Kar Kraft's workshops in a suburb of Detroit.
(Collins Collection)

The prototype with the first stainless panels in place.

One of the first gullwing doors under construction.

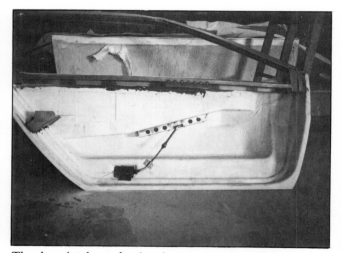

The door latch mechanism in a prototype gullwing door.

Front subframe with the suspension and steering rack.

Making the SAE measurements.

A roof cage or "spider" would support the gullwings.

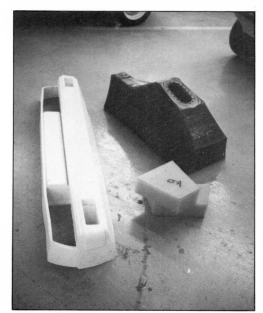
Plastic front-end cap & central fuel cell . . .

First the basic engine subframe was constructed...

. . . then the 4-cylinder Citroën installed.

All the sheetmetal and subframes have been added.

Bill Collins "driving" the uncompleted first prototype.

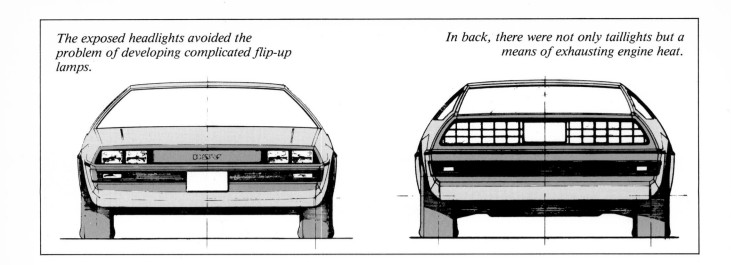

The exposed headlights avoided the problem of developing complicated flip-up lamps.

In back, there were not only taillights but a means of exhausting engine heat.

the tooling for the De Lorean underbody. This required making a buck with a surface that was exactly as a finished piece should look in reverse, and then producing a fiberglass body half. While the underbody was being developed, the subframes also had to be fabricated, and one month led to the next into 1976.

Citroën Says Goodbye

Altogether it took a year building the first prototype, which first ran in October, 1976. But by then there had already been another fundamental change in the ingredients. Although the Citroën engine/ transmission made a neat and proven package, the

Detail drawing shows all measurements with the rear-engine Renault drivetrain.

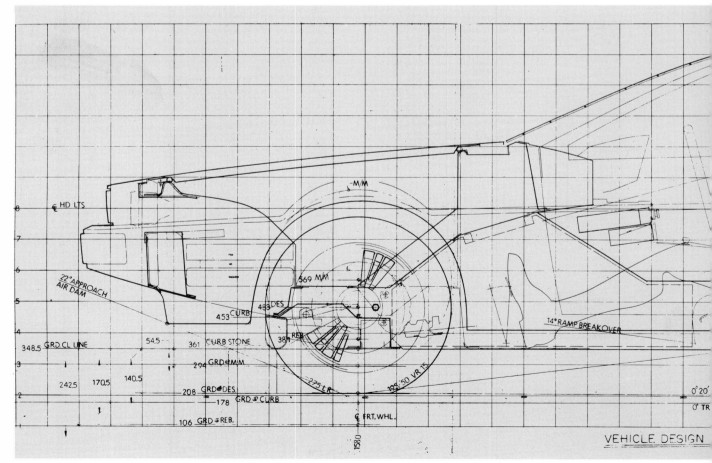

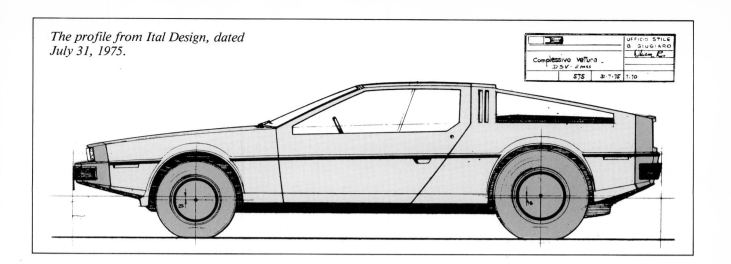

The profile from Ital Design, dated July 31, 1975.

1985-cc engine's 102 horsepower were obviously insufficient for a Grand Touring car. To make matters worse, the engine was only offered with either a 4-speed manual or 3-speed automatic transmission, with no 5-speed manual gearbox. The answer was to turbocharge the 4-cylinder powerplant. George Taylor, president of Citroën, visited the company in the summer of 1976 to discuss De Lorean buying the CX 2000 powertrain. When he heard of the plans to turbocharge the engine, Taylor balked and suggested the Americans find another engine. The Citroën may have been somewhat anemic, but it was a compact unit

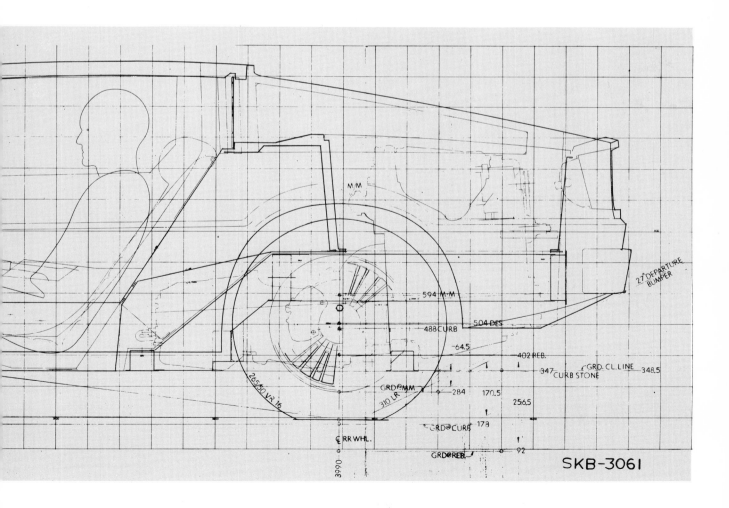

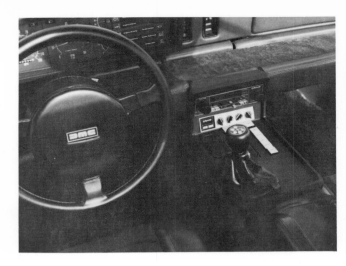

The De Lorean was designed to be a safety car and the interior had several features to back up the claim. The thick steering wheel pad and the wide knee bar were part of the "passive" safety equipment meant to protect a driver and passenger even if they weren't wearing safety belts. In the center console was a racing-type fuel cell to cut after-crash fire danger.
(Collins)

that would fit in the De Lorean as a mid-engine car. This is quite desirable from a weight distribution standpoint, and it was going to be difficult to find a replacement drivetrain that would do the same.

In fact, other than having the same basic styling, the car that rolled out of Kar Kraft in October, 1976, would be totally different from the De Lorean that would go into production four years later. There wasn't much that could be learned from it, but then Collins never had a chance anyway. Almost immediately, the car was snatched up by C. R. "Dick" Brown and the sales department to become a selling tool to investors. It made its public debut in New Orleans in March, 1977, at the National Automobile Dealers Association meeting, where De Lorean kicked off the campaign to sign up dealer/investors. If there wasn't more money found soon the De Lorean DMC-12, good, bad or mediocre, wasn't going to be produced. This was because a second attempt to raise money in the spring of 1976 had failed.

This try was a joint effort by De Lorean and Tom Fatjo of Criterion Capital Corporation in Houston, Texas. Bill Collins recalls, "We went back and forth with them from March until the end of the summer and literally spent every week in Houston." In the end it came to nothing gained, and, in fact, the temporary ties with Criterion cost DMC 75,000 shares of common stock, valued at the time at $10 per share, which had to be paid to Criterion.

Meet The Press

In addition to being paraded around to raise capital, the De Lorean was presented to the major automotive magazines. John Dinkel, then *Road & Track's* Engineering Editor, and I had a chance to see, touch, photograph, ask about, but not drive the first prototype.

Naturally the De Lorean was quite impressive

when we first saw it. The design was still fresh then, and the stainless steel was stunning. Jerry Williamson and the crew that carted the car from show to show had its preparation down to an art and so it was in its prime when I had a chance to photograph it. The exterior styling was much as it is today and only Giugiaro's minor retuning of the shape would change before production. The Citroën inline-4 nestled in the mid-engine position very nicely.

What was significantly different about the first prototype and later De Loreans was the interior. When Giugiaro designed the interior, the DMC-12 was still meant to be a safety car, and so a very prominent feature of the inside is the full-width knee bar. Collins and Giugiaro had had one of their few points of disagreement on this detail, but in the end it looked like an integral part of the interior. A medium brown leather covered the seats, which had center inserts of velour. These seats were much flatter than the production models, not offering the comfort and support of the more rounded production seats. There was a massive center console, and it was to house the fuel tank, which would have a foam-filled racing type fuel cell. On the console were not only the shift lever, but also the controls for heating/ventilation/air conditioning—the latter would be standard equipment—and the radio. The emergency brake handle was disguised as what looked like the cover to a console storage bin.

Ahead of the driver was a black steering wheel with a fat center that was meant to contain an air bag. On the instrument panel was a full set of very attractive Stewart-Warner gauges monitoring engine rpm, speed, volts, coolant temperature, oil pressure and fuel level. Warning lights would respond to any other problems that might arise. They were part of a central warning system that would check various fluid levels, temperatures and warn of low brake pad thickness,

What do these two cars have in common? Both the first De Lorean prototype and the 1936 Ford are skinned with stainless steel. The Ford was done by Allegheny Ludlum to promote the virtue of stainless as a body material. (DMC)

though it was suspected this last feature wouldn't show up on the early production cars. Turn signals, high beam switch and windshield wiper/washer functions were handled with a stalk on the left side of the steering column.

Ahead of the passenger compartment was the trunk, which was as nicely carpeted as the interior. Missing was a spare tire. "I haven't solved that problem yet," Collins chuckled.

The engineer's humor came through again when asked about the handling characteristics of the De Lorean. "Mike and I spent a lot of time talking about the basic handling parameters . . . so the objective we had was that no magazine writer was ever going to flip it over." The goal was not to create a race car, but a gentleman's sports car. The front and rear suspension had the same basic ingredients: upper and lower A-arms, coil springs, tube shock absorbers and an anti-roll bar. It was planned to have adjustable air shocks at the front to help trim the car when there was

luggage in the nose. Bendix European disc brake calipers were used with discs made by Pocobello; calipers are complex and expensive and should be bought from an outside supplier, while discs are relatively easy to manufacture. As previously noted, the rack and pinion steering in this first prototype came from a Ford Pinto, and a prominent feature was the large Pirelli P7 tires, 195/50VR-15's at the front and 265/50VR-16's in back mounted on, respectively, 6 x 15-in. and 8 x 16-in. cast aluminum alloy wheels.

With this prototype done and a second one on the way, Collins commented to Dinkel and myself in early 1977 that the second prototype should be ready by July. Beginning in January, 1978, he would start work on an additional 10 prototypes to be used for durability and crash testing. Things didn't go that smoothly.

3

The Serious Money

ALL THE CHANGES to be made constructing the second prototype meant Bill Collins would have to start anew on several aspects of the DMC-12. The first prototype now went "on the road" to awe and inspire investors, kicking off the campaign to recruit dealers at the National Automobile Dealers Association (NADA) meeting in March, 1977, in New Orleans. Bill Collins went, at least metaphorically, back to the drawing board.

The NADA's convention was picked to debut the De Lorean because the new investment program involved not only raising money, but also attracting dealerships. The basic plan was quite simple. To become a De Lorean dealer you had to be an established automobile dealer willing to buy $25,000 in DMC common stock. In addition to sending mechanics to a De Lorean service school, buying or renting proper signs and providing showroom facilities, the dealer then had to agree to buy a certain number of cars, a figure that was determined dealer by dealer. De Lorean hoped to sign 400 dealers for an additional $10,000,000.

Doom And Gloom From The SEC

The preliminary prospectus for this stock offering, dated January 28, 1977, was filled with dire warnings for potential dealers. On its cover was the sentence, "This investment involves a high degree of risk and should be considered only by those who can afford a total loss of such investment." It went on to point out that DMC had no operating history, no revenues and no assets other than the rights to the work that had already been done on the car. After mentioning the failure of any automotive company to get started in the U.S. in many years, the prospectus added, among other things, that the De Lorean would have a limited market, there were no manufacturing facilities, no marketing or sales organization, that the automobile was only in the early developmental

C.R. "Dick" Brown played a critical part in helping raise DMC's key dealer funding. (DMC)

stages and that a great deal of the chance for success of the De Lorean depended on just a few men. Exciting reading.

On The Road Again

The dealer sales program was known within the company as the John De Lorean and Dick Brown Traveling Road Show, and was exhausting for

On tour in 1978 to impress potential investors, first prototype poses in front of Bonaventure Hotel in Los Angeles. (DMC)

The prototype probably racked up countless miles being loaded and unloaded from trucks. (Collins)

everyone involved. It was modeled on the way Dick Brown formed the Mazda dealer organization. Jerry Williamson, who is now an independent marketing consultant in California, was a part of the show, and described for us how it worked.

The shows were always held in very good to excellent hotels, and the tone was deliberately low key. Automobile dealers were the target, and while there were occasions when they were contacted ahead of time by letter or telegram, they were usually invited by phone. The De Lorean crew would hustle back to their rooms after the day's dog-and-pony show, grab the yellow pages and begin calling prospective dealers in upcoming cities on the tour. There were follow-up calls and checklists to make sure who would be there. This may sound rather haphazard, but Williamson says it proved to be sensible and very effective. The bigger, more aggressive dealers (i.e. the ones most likely to come. . .and have the money) were usually the ones with the biggest ads in the yellow pages, although nearly every dealer in the next town was contacted.

The prototype was the centerpiece of the show.

The car and all the necessary audio-visual equipment was loaded in a large truck, which was driven from city to city, often 700 miles overnight, to be at the next show. Williamson and another man, Larry Taylor at one point and Robbie Hilton later on, would get to the next hotel and begin to unload the car and equipment. If needed, the prototype was impeccably detailed and the stainless steel scratch-brushed.

The physical arrangement of the meeting room was always the same, unless there was to be an unusually large crowd. The guests were seated at a U-shaped table that opened toward a projection screen, but the car itself was hidden out of view until after all the presentations. Only then would it be revealed to the now thoroughly interested crowd. Shades of Gypsy Rose Lee.

John De Lorean attended quite a few of these meetings, hedgehopping in Boeing 737's all over the country, greeting the dealers after each meeting and answering questions. C.R. "Dick" Brown was the main speaker. He would also fly from one city to the next and was the one who gave the Securities Exchange Commission-approved sales spiel word-for-word, unable to vary it 10 words from beginning to end. There was an introduction, a slide show, a narrative and then a film, followed by an open forum and a question and answer session.

Say It With Music

At first the SEC balked at the idea of DMC using slides or a movie in their attempt to raise capital. Then a show was devised that followed the carefully couched words of the prospectus; no claims were made and all adjectives and superlatives were eliminated. The movie had also been a problem with the SEC and it too had to avoid any sort of hype. Williamson produced the movie and it was photographed by Bob Bagley, who had worked with Bruce Brown in his famous surfing and motorcycle movies. They got around potential SEC objections by using no words, only music. The car speeds through picturesque Ortega Canyon, south of Newport Beach, California, and the helicopter shots of the car with the background music emphasize the De Lorean "follow the dream" theme. Williamson suspects that the film was more effective with only music and dynamic visuals. On occasion dealers would stand and applaud when the movie had finished.

By his estimates, Williamson figures that 30 percent of the dealers called would attend the meeting and almost five percent of those would sign with De Lorean. Rarely would a dealer leave in the middle of the meeting, but maybe 10 percent were ready to ridicule the idea. However, 40 percent were willing to give John De Lorean the benefit of the doubt and the other 50 were solidly behind him . . . though in the end it was the same five percent who signed. To bring their willingness to part with the required $25,000 back into perspective once again, remember that many of these dealers had benefited substantially—or seen others do so—from John De Lorean's successful years at Pontiac and Chevrolet. The audiences didn't vary that much from city to city, car dealers being car dealers, though Williamson remembers the reception in Chicago being particularly good.

"It was all handled very tastefully." Williamson adds, "we never tried to put on an officious air, we always looked a little bit hungry and we never, never tried to hype them with liquor . . . only Cokes, coffee, tea and danish rolls. And in the end we had people who would write us a $25,000 check on the spot. That was the advertising budget for one month for some of those guys, and look at the traffic this car would attract. Just on the basis of the car sitting on the showroom floor it was worth their money."

There is one curious note to all this, involving John De Lorean. Several of the participants in the road show comment that De Lorean had the embarrassing habit of exaggerating such things as his business accomplishments, or the number of exotic cars he'd owned—even when those around him were aware of what he had and hadn't done. The braggadocio came as a surprise to the followers of the ethical car builder, but in retrospect is in keeping with his entrepreneurial temperament and need to win people's confidence.

The Key To The Whole Project

All that chasing around the country didn't bring the 400 dealers hoped for, but 158 had signed by October 31, 1977. More would ante up later for a total of 343, with 173 of those also being General Motors dealers. These dealers provided $8.2 million in capital, but their importance went well beyond the money they contributed. For one thing, it was, in some estimations (not all—see Bruce McWilliams' comments in Chapter 10) a good set of dealers for De Lorean, because the sort of men willing to bet $25,000 on De Lorean's promise were the kind of aggressive dealers who would probably end up doing the best sales job for the car. Any dealership on shaky ground, either financially or in attitude, wasn't going to be on the list. Crucially important, without this large, quality dealer body in place there probably wouldn't have been a city, state or country willing to financially back the De Lorean factory.

John De Lorean notes, "The dealers were really the key to our whole project. When you got all through, the only real credibility we had was that a certain number of dealers had been willing to make an investment in the project and to commit to purchase cars as time went by . . . nothing else really gave it substance." So even though it fell short of the ultimate target, in the end the John De Lorean and Dick Brown Traveling Show worked very nicely indeed.

There was another group of DMC investors, these

Television star Johnny Carson was an early investor in the De Lorean Motor Company, putting up $500,000, for which he was given not only a De Lorean Sports Car, but a chance to designate a representative as a Director of the company. When he picked up his car, the alternator failed as he was driving home. (DMC)

being individuals, who together brought in another $1.2 million. The most famous is television star Johnny Carson, who added $500,000 fairly early in the game. As if to counter the early lack of enthusiasm for De Lorean's project by their industry, 15 executives from the investment firm of Merrill Lynch put in $475,000 between them. One of the men likened seeing the De Lorean prototype to being a little boy in a toy store.

Re-Engineering For Renault

One of the first problems with the second prototype would be replacing the Citroën engine. There weren't many possibilities, but easily the best was the single overhead camshaft V-6 developed and manufactured jointly by Peugeot, Renault and Volvo in Douvrain, France. Sold in 2.6- and 2.8-liter forms, the engine had been certified for U.S. emissions in the Peugeot 604 and the Volvo 260 series. That meant the De Lorean, an automobile weighing less than either the Peugeot or Volvo, would only have to run a 5,000-mile certification check for emissions, rather than the expensive and time-consuming 50,000-mile emissions durability tests. Both the Peugeot and Volvo are front-engine, rear-wheel-drive cars, but Renault uses the engine in their front-wheel-drive 30. Douvrain would be able to produce an engine with the emissions equipment of the Peugeot and Volvo but with the block of a Renault 30. This block meant the engine would bolt right up to Renault's front-drive transaxle, which now became a rear-drive transaxle as the entire unit was shifted to the back of the car and rotated 180 degrees, as it is in the Renault Alpine A310. Collins was happy with the choice because he'd worked with Renault in late 1974 when DMC was doing some consulting work with Renault on their R5, and he'd been impressed with their engineers.

This engine swap meant the second prototype

Renault's Alpine A310 V-6 has the Douvrain engine mounted behind the rear axle. This made the Alpine an ideal test car for the De Lorean drivetrain, and one Alpine was converted to an automatic transmission. (Renault)

would have to be re-engineered for the new engine and take another step forward in detail design for production. Collins discussed the matter with Pocobello and they both decided it would be best if the project was moved to a larger firm. DMC had also gotten the $3.5 million from the Sports Car Partnership to finance this more ambitious move and, with John De Lorean's urging, the scene moved to another Detroit firm, Creative Industries.

The first job was to redesign the back portion of the plastic underbody for the Renault drivetrain. To have kept the mid-engine layout by turning the rather tall Renault engine around would have resulted in a car that was too long. By retaining the front-wheel-drive drivetrain and moving it rearward this length

The Alpine A310 is built in Dieppe by a division of Renault. The body is made of fiberglass and the car was first introduced in 1971 with a 4-cylinder engine. The V-6 version was introduced in 1976. (Lamm)

problem was solved and, as a side benefit, they picked up added space behind the seats, because the Citroen engine was right behind the bulkhead. The sacrifice was making the De Lorean into a rear-engine car, which would be more difficult to develop into a fine-handling sports car.

With the decision to use the Renault V-6, Collins needed to find a way to develop their edition of the engine and transaxle. The ideal vehicle was Renault's Alpine A310 V-6. This is a fiberglass-body sports car built in Dieppe, France by Alpine, a subsidiary of Renault that is responsible for many of the sport versions of the parent corporation's cars. The sleek, Trevor Fiore-designed sports car was introduced at the Geneva Auto Show in 1971 and five years later

re-introduced with the V-6 positioned behind the rear axle. DMC eventually owned four of the French sport cars as development cars, including one converted to use an automatic transmission, a combination not built by Alpine.

Job 1—A Moving Target

While Creative Industries was working on the second car, Collins was beginning to add to his staff, hiring Peter Giacobbi for what would be a short stint as Chief Engineer. Joe Sahutske began as a designer/draftsman. Bob Manion left Chrysler to do the electrics of the De Lorean. In addition to building this car, they were also trying to establish the car's various components—air conditioning, instrument cluster, etc.—and who would supply them. All of this decision making and sourcing was aimed at the date of first production, known in Detroit as Job 1, but the date was proving to be a moving target. This was a new, unexpected experience for Collins: "When building a car you can always sit down and say, okay, this is the Job 1 date if everything goes along all right, and this means getting the money, which you don't worry about in the end because at GM you just have the money approved. At De Lorean we always had the spectre of having to raise more money and that always made things change."

As 1977 moved on, Collins wasn't too happy with Creative, a situation he now wraps up merely by saying they didn't provide the engineering services he'd expected. "The time at Creative was not a good time. It didn't work out the way I wanted it to. Mike Pocobello and Chuck Mountain are perfectionists at making parts fit right and look right and there wasn't anything like that at Creative." John De Lorean concurs with Collins, adding, "We found that as a little guy, thinly financed, we got short shrift, so to say." The De Lorean Motor Company was still short of

Bill Collins (left) with the basic underbody used for the first two De Lorean prototypes. It was planned that this part of the car would be made by a process called Elastic Reservoir Molding, for which DMC owned the rights. After development problems with ERM the underbodies had to be made of fiberglass. (Ludvigsen)

A mock-up of the second car's rear subframe. (Ludvigsen)

Second prototype at Creative Industries. (Collins)

engineering staff, and compounding this, Collins' time was diluted to help raise money and look at potential plant sites.

While all the changes needed to fit the V-6 in the De Lorean were being made at Creative, Collins was beginning to contact outside suppliers, one being Grumman Aerospace. The original De Lorean design had its steel roof "spider" attached to the fiberglass underbody and that spider became a platform for the heavy gullwing doors. Collins would have preferred a non-metallic spider to save weight and wondered if Grumman could do the spider in ERM with a material such as carbon fiber for added strength.

Making The Gullwings Work

Grumman was looking for the answer to this problem when Collins also mentioned that he hadn't yet found a truly satisfactory means of getting the gullwing doors up smoothly and with minimal effort. "The first one that Mike built," Collins explains, "had four little 1/8-inch diameter rods that went forward

into a block of steel, sort of welded in there, and then four that went back the other way. It was always making noise and one of the bars would slip and then it wouldn't work. So I said, 'I need a bar that is about 32 inches long that I can mount back in the roll bar and then forward that will open this heavy door.' Their development guy, Art August, said, 'Let me give that to our (he called them) Dr. Phoo-phoos, and see what they can do.'" What Grumman had was a cryogenically stressed torsion bar. They put the bar, which has been stretched and straightened, in liquid nitrogen—at minus 320 degrees Fahrenheit—and twist it through 10 revolutions. The grain structure of the bar is rearranged and during the process it gets neither smaller in diameter nor shorter. Said to be good for 50,000 opening and closing cycles without losing strength, Grumman's "crysotwist" bar became the ideal torsion bar for the De Lorean doors. The same bar was used in the production De Lorean, produced by the Unbrako division of SPS Technologies.

There were other supplier contacts made during

Prototypes number one and two at the left, with the Ital Design epo-wood styling mock-up. (Jerry Williamson Collection)

this time. AC Spark Plug was contracted to do the instrument cluster. General Motors' Harrison Division agreed to produce the car's heater/air conditioner. One project that was petering out, however, was the use of ERM. Collins was still interested, but it was becoming obvious that hard steel tools, not the less expensive resin dies, would be needed, so ERM was forced into the future.

As the second De Lorean prototype came closer to what would be a December, 1977, completion, it was becoming still more obvious things weren't working out as planned. The day when the second car was finally rolled out "was not a good day" for Collins.

Nonetheless, the chance to build additional prototypes was coming quickly, thanks to the completion of the first dealer offering at the end of October in which 158 dealers contributed their $25,000 each for $3,750,000. In those early months of 1978, Mike Pocobello was doing some development on the second car such as structural work, front suspension analysis, emissions and fuel economy runs and cooling tests. Zora-Arkus Duntov, the man in charge of the Chevrolet Corvette until his retirement in 1975, also worked with Collins as a consultant.

In early summer, 1978, during a development trip to Phoenix where the car was undergoing heating and cooling runs, Colin Chapman and Mike Kimberley of Lotus Cars, Ltd. first came to see the DMC-12 at the invitation of John De Lorean. Later, they said the car was abominable, a point Collins wouldn't argue too strongly, because he was also disappointed with the results of this second attempt.

Getting The Serious Money

As 1978 moved on, there were other problems as important as developing the DMC-12, the main ones being to find a place and the capital to build the car. All the sources mentioned so far, excluding any money

De Lorean may have added himself—some would claim he put in no cash—brought in enough to cover much of the cost of developing the car and distribution system, but it wouldn't pay to get the car manufactured. Now we get to the truly serious amounts of money . . . and that is tied directly to the story of how the De Lorean came to be built in Northern Ireland.

A number of cities, states and countries wanted the De Lorean factory. There was glamor to having this newest automobile built locally, but there were also a great number of jobs to be filled and so the prospect appealed to any locale with high unemployment. That's what had drawn New Brunswick, Canada into the Bricklin project. When it was obvious the De Lorean would, in fact, be built, rumors began as to where the factory would be located. Mayor Coleman Young of Detroit wanted it in the Motor City. There were overtures from Texas, Pennsylvania, Alabama and Kansas. France was interested, as were Portugal and Spain.

Most serious of this early group was Puerto Rico. Suffering from unemployment, this U.S. Commonwealth island in the West Indian Ocean had just the location for DMC. Ramey Air Force Base, built for the Strategic Air Command, was now abandoned and the local jobless rate was 30 percent. Not only were there huge hangars that could be made into factories, but the runways would make an excellent test track. It was estimated that the factory would be around 500,000 square feet and employ some 2,000 local workers. There were convenient local harbors for shipping, but De Lorean, ever alert to capture the imagination, talked of using the base to fly his automobiles to the States in Boeing 747's modified for just that purpose. All Puerto Rico needed to do was provide—with help from the U.S. government—some $65 million.

"An Act Of Treason"

Talks between Puerto Rico and De Lorean had begun in March, 1977, and eventually the U.S. Economic Development Administration and the Farmers Home Administration had agreed to guarantee some $40 million in loans for the project. It appeared that the Puerto Rican government would lend another $17.7 million to De Lorean and give a $3 million grant to help train workers. It was during the summer, 1978, that these final talks were taking place —one insider claims the Puerto Ricans were dragging their feet—when quite abruptly John De Lorean signed with the government of Northern Ireland to build the car in Belfast. Governor Carlos Romero-Barcelo of Puerto Rico was furious and threatened "possible legal action." De Lorean's move was even termed an "act of treason." But it was too late.

Puerto Rico had known, of course, that even after the island and the car company had gotten down to serious talks De Lorean was meeting with representatives from other potential plant sites. One of those groups had come from the Republic of Ireland, and a deputation of 12 men from there viewed the investor presentation in Houston. That summer they came back with an offer, but in the end, the Northern Irish government—backed by Great Britain's Labour Party

De Lorean wanted to ship his cars from Puerto Rico in 747s; the lounge area was for owners going to visit the factory.

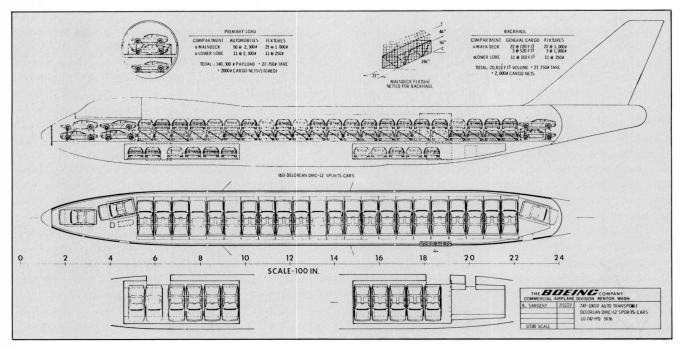

government—offered a proposal that outdid all others . . . and the project moved to Belfast.

According to John De Lorean, both Puerto Rico and the Republic of Ireland had been eliminated before DMC signed with Northern Ireland. In Puerto Rico, "We got into an impossible situation in that the only piece of ground we were permitted to build a factory on was a piece of the old Ramey Air Force Base." It seems the base was built in a rush during World War II and the government never got the normal eminent domain clearance to build, but ". . . just went and broomed all these 500 farmers off the land, built the air base and then the ones that kicked and protested, I assume they did something with them. In any event, they never had clear title." When the air base was returned to Puerto Rico the government still didn't have clear title to all the land.

When it came time to cover the question of the De Lorean factory in Puerto Rico, the Government Development Bank could only pass on the limited title they held from the U.S. government. De Lorean asked the governor to take the land under eminent domain or to buy another piece of land. According to De Lorean, the governor said, "No, we can't do that as it was all part of the enabling legislation, it's got to be here (the air force base). I can't condemn it because if I do that the poor people of Puerto Rico will think I'm using my governmental powers to steal their land. And so we wound up with not Catch-22, but Catch 222."

Then there was the bid from the Republic of Ireland. They also had a factory: "It was a plant in Limerick, which is near the Shannon Airport. It had 250,000 square feet, really a beautiful facility that they wanted us to use. It was a plant that had been the subject of tremendous labor problems over a long period of time and at one point the manager was kidnapped." When DMC's auditors looked into the factory deal,

however, ". . . we found that they were asking us to pay a price that was far more than the value of the property and with a much higher interest rate." Overpaying for a factory was the last thing the fledgling company could afford to do.

There was one other serious possibility, De Lorean relates, ". . . the chance of going back to Detroit if we could get the federal government to agree to make the funding available in Detroit. They wouldn't do that as long as there was an act of consideration of Puerto Rico."

"So we did the best thing we could do," De Lorean commented in mid-1982 about choosing Northern Ireland, "and I've never been unhappy with it."

The Payoff: $177,141,200

John De Lorean had, of course, been playing a game of high-finance brinksmanship with all the suitors. It was a necessary gambit, the stakes were enormous, and here's what he got for his efforts: The two governmental organizations that dealt with De Lorean were the Northern Ireland Development Agency and the Department of Commerce. When the agreement was signed on July 28, 1978, the first amount guaranteed De Lorean was up to $112,971,200. That broke down into $36,363,600 of equity investment, $55,973,600 in grants and $20,634,000 in loans. Later there was another loan, this one of $28,980,000, and the DOC guaranteed another $35,190,000 in loans through banks.

The $36 million figure represents the Irish investment in De Lorean Motors Limited—the arm of the De Lorean Motor Co. established to manufacture the car—and for it they received all that division's Class A stock, some 17,757,000 shares.

Among the grants were $14,927,000 to cover half the cost of construction of the factory. A loan covered the other half of that expense. Another $14,787,500

was used to meet half the price of buying and installing the machinery and equipment. A later grant paid
for the other half. Just over $10 million paid for tool-
ing that had to be built and intalled in the factories
of some of the companies making parts for De Lorean.
There were other grants guaranteed on the basis of the
number of employees on the payroll, just as there were
penalties on De Lorean's part if a certain number of
employees were not working by certain dates.

Other loans to De Lorean included $35,707,500,
which covered the working capital needed to operate
the company until production could begin. The bank
loans guaranteed by DOC were intended to keep the
company in business while the sales of cars grew.

For the British money, Northern Ireland got the
De Lorean project. With that came over 2,500 jobs
in an area hurting because of unemployment, though
at a cost many Englishmen—who were in effect paying the bill—thought was too high. (It was a subject
that came up more than once in the British Parliament
and was at one time at the heart of a purported scandal considered serious enough to arouse the interest
of Scotland Yard. In the end, John De Lorean was
cleared. There was also bitterness in British automotive
circles that several small specialist firms such as Pan-
ther Westwinds were allowed to go under and could
get no government help, while an outsider such as
De Lorean could. John De Lorean's lifestyle, and the
flamboyant—and expensive—manner in which he
operated his company were constantly called into question by the British.)

On The Road Again: Part II

Right about this time the Great DMC Investment
Show got back on the road to pitch the third major
group of investors. These were to be the proposed 125
members of the De Lorean Research Limited Partnership, which was established (closed) on September 22,
1978. This was a matter of taking another run at heavy
hitters, aiming at investors with incomes of $500,000
or more. De Lorean prevailed upon Oppenheimer &
Co., Inc., the well-known investment banking company, to sell the partnership units for them, and the
same program put on for dealers was also done for
interested investors. The Oppenheimer move and the
second drive for dealers overlapped somewhat, and
in some cities there would be a dealer show in the
morning and an Oppenheimer show that afternoon.

For this offering there was no set amount that
had to be put up by any investor, but the numbers
were huge, as were the potential tax benefits for those
putting their money into DMC, because again the
money raised by this offering was earmarked for
research and development. And again their investment
was covered, in a sense, because DMC, which had
recovered the rights to the sports car and its development by "buying out" the De Lorean Sports Car Partnership, now transferred those rights to the Research
Limited Partnership. The list of options for DMC and
the Partnership were many, from one day buying the
partners' interests—as DMC did with the original
partnership—to eventually paying royalties to the new
investors for each car sold. In the end there was an
additional $18,752,500 brought in, though after Op-
penheimer's fees were subtracted the actual amount
that went into DMC coffers was closer to $15,500,000.

Both partnerships were based on hard-nosed
economics, with tax benefits that meant the partners
wouldn't really lose even if the company went belly-
up. If DMC had succeeded, the investors would have
made a great deal of money, but unfortunately it now
appears that these investors, along with so many
others, will have to exercise the tax benefit side of
their investment.

COLOR SALON #1
Styling and Prototype

Italian stylist Giugiaro worked up a great many ideas based on the design parameters he was given in 1975, as shown by the sketches. The front end at right most closely resembles the production car. Below are more front end variations, with the associated side view beneath in the 2nd row. Still more variations are shown in the 3rd row.

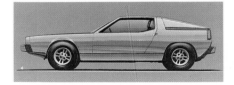

At left, front and rear sketches of "might have beens."

The rear styling of this car was the basis for the full-scale model.

Ital Design built the first full-scale model by lathering this wooden framework with a special epoxy plaster, then precisely sculpting the final contours. (DMC)

This is the final epo-wood styling model built by Ital Design. Complete in every detail, it was shipped to Detroit to serve as the basis for building the first prototype. (DMC)

Milford Fabricating stamped out the first prototype's stainless panels based on the pine-die model carved out by Design Caucus (below).

Who's Going To Pay For All This???

The first money-raising effort was a program put together in October, 1975, by the firm of Gregg & Wardell in New York City to form a limited partnership, with the ante $100,000 per partner. Below is reproduced a slide from a DMC presentation showing what would happen to the investor's money, and in fact the partners' interest was traded for $8 per share cumulative convertible preferred stock on October 31, 1977. Another DMC slide shows the financial scenario envisioned in early 1976. The $10 million dealer investment fell short (only 158 signed up initially for $3.8 million) but ultimately there were 343. The proposed $45 million public offering never happened, but a De Lorean Research limited partnership did raise $15.5 million (after fees) in September, 1978. By then the British had stepped up to the bar with what would total $171 million.

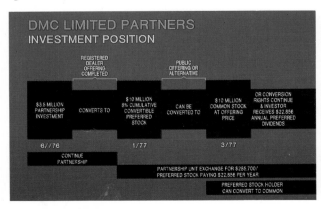

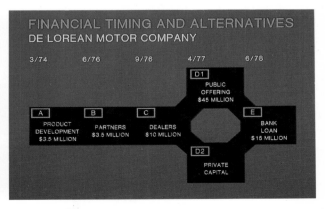

Three views of the first De Lorean prototype, the "DMC-12" as it was then known. The public debut was in March, 1977, at the National Automobile Dealer Association (NADA) convention in New Orleans. (DMC)

Live the dream indeed. Clothed in stainless steel and ready to drive away, the prototype raised great hopes among enthusiasts. (Lamm)

The hard-edged treatment by Giugiaro shows the stainless steel to superb advantage in crisp, clean lines. (Lamm)

Interior of first prototype differs markedly from final car, with massive center console housing safety fuel cell, full width safety knee bar, air bag container in the steering wheel center, and seats with less padding and support. Brown leather was a better choice than the production car's black hole of Calcutta. (DMC)

*These 1975 DMC drawings show the Ford V-6
incorporated in a rear-engine design, but by the time
construction of the prototype began in October, this
engine had been dropped in favor of the 4-cylinder,
1985 cc Citroën 2000 CX engine/transmission.*
(Bill Collins Collection)

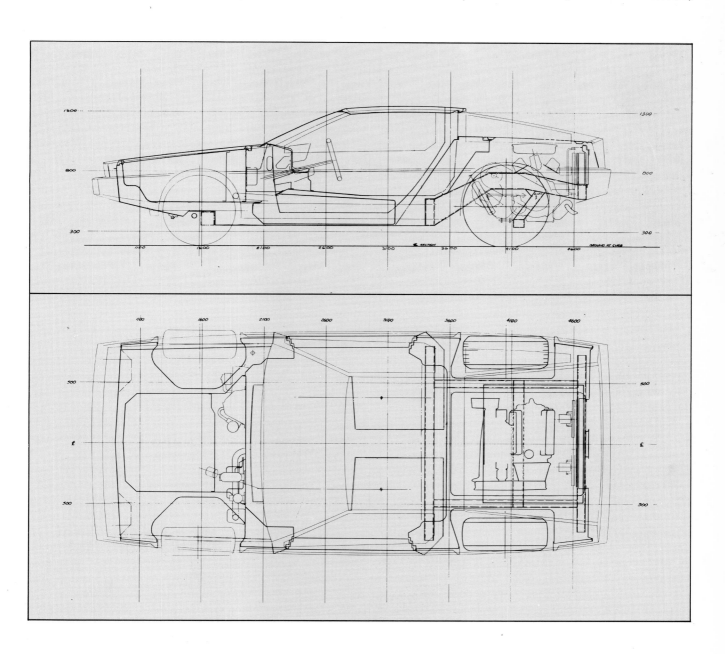

4

Lotus Takes The Wheel

WHEN THE PLAN TO BUILD the De Lorean in Puerto Rico evaporated with the decision to sign with Northern Ireland, sourcing parts for the car became a new problem. Many of these pieces would now have to come from Europe, and Collins agreed it was necessary to move the engineering department to England, nearer to their suppliers. So Collins and Alan Cross, an ex-Ford, ex-Bricklin engineer and expatriate Englishman, went to Great Britain to find a place to establish the De Lorean engineering center. Coventry appeared to be the logical choice. The city is in England's Midlands and, in a sense, is England's Detroit, with not only automobile companies such as Jaguar and (then) Chrysler, but also a great number of automotive parts suppliers. Now, however, came another change, for before Bill Collins could make arrangements to establish his staff in Coventry, John De Lorean signed with Lotus to develop the DMC-12. The tab for the development work was $12.5 million, to be funneled from Switzerland through a Panama-registered company called General Products Development Services, Inc.

This move to Lotus wasn't a surprise for Collins, who knew De Lorean was working on a plan to establish a DMC/Lotus engineering center in the manner of Porsche, with the intent to do consulting work to "the world." As De Lorean explains, "We went through the available engineering resources (in Europe) and we had talked to Lotus early on (however) they refused to take our project because they didn't think we had enough money to finish it. In any event, we went through Jensen, Aston Martin and whatever . . . there aren't many independent engineering organizations over there. We'd gone through all of those and we finally got into a situation where we had accepted the contract from the Northern Ireland government and we'd lost 90 days trying to find an

engineering resource. . . . If we didn't get going pretty quickly we'd probably have our agreement terminated. We'd gone to Porsche and they wanted two years more than Lotus. Porsche has, of course, incredibly talented engineers, but they wanted those two years, which was intolerable by the government's timetable. We just couldn't wait that long."

Indeed that was true, for it was now November, 1978, and Collins had to rush to get his staff to Lotus' headquarters in Norwich, 100 miles northeast of London in the Norfolk district. Cross and his family moved, as did chief draftsman Joe Sahutske and his family, and the expert on U.S. government emissions and safety regulations, Steve Matson, who had worked with Cross at Bricklin. Bob Manion was also scheduled to move. They were all transferred to furnished houses near Norwich.

Kept At Arm's Length

Almost from the start, relations between Lotus and the De Lorean group were chilly. As Collins remembers it, "I thought it was incumbent upon me to provide Lotus with every bit of knowledge that we could, all the test work we'd done, all our design work and the guys who had worked on it. Well, they treated us so shabbily you wouldn't believe it."

Collins and company were installed in Ketteringham Hall, a lovely and stately manor house which was Jimmy Stewart's command center when he served with the U.S. Army Air Corps during World War II. Though it looks like a set from a BBC Masterpiece Theater production, "Ket Hall" is now the Lotus think tank. The De Lorean contingent was set up in the old chapel.

Despite (because of??) their close proximity to the Lotus people, they were kept at arm's length. Collins describes his attempts to talk with Chapman about the De Lorean: "Chapman would talk with you

The Lotus/De Lorean brain trust. Clockwise from John De Lorean; Fred Bushell (now head of Lotus), Colin Chapman, Eugene Cafiero, Mike Kimberley and Colin Spooner. Beginning in November 1978, Group Lotus had the De Lorean ready for production in just 25 months. (Tony Howarth for Woodfin Camp & Associates)

and he'd say 'talk with each other and we'll get this thing done sooner or later.' But just to ask when they would get something started I had to trap him. I'd call his office at Ketteringham Hall and they'd say they weren't sure where he was. So then I'd call Tony Rudd's or Mike Kimberley's secretary and she'd say, 'Oh, Mike's tied up with the Chairman [as Chapman is known—Ed.]' and I'd think, 'Aha, I know where he is. . . .' Since I was a director of the Northern Ireland company I was allowed to park in the director's garage. I'd park in there and slip into the back door of the building. Chapman would be in a meeting, so I'd wait outside until he was finished and then I'd nail him." Collins adds, "It seemed like an incredibly childish and unprofessional game for grown men to be playing with so much work to be done—not the way GM operates!"

John De Lorean sees it differently. "When we went to Lotus it was originally at his (Bill Collins') recommendation. He said, 'Look, I can't do it any other way, we've got to or we're going to lose the contract.' So we went into Lotus and then he expected Colin Chapman to be like one of his staff engineers at Pontiac and, of course, Colin is a different sort of guy. He's very much an individual, and they crossed swords almost from day number one. . . ."

Eventually the De Lorean staff was moved to a small building behind a huge former hangar that was to become the project center for the De Lorean. Collins and staff had little to do . . . and then one day they saw the Lotus evaluation of the second De Lorean prototype, which had been shipped to Hethel. Dubbed "War and Peace," the thick document was very critical of the car. Collins was "mad as hell." He was willing to admit to the car's shortcomings, but felt the report was unfair. He remembers John De Lorean saying to him, "Relax, everything's going to be fine." Collins wasn't so certain.

Collins Resigns

Engineering may be based on hard rules and mathematics, but that doesn't mean a pair of creative engineers can't disagree with all the passion of two artists. Collins and Chapman each had their ways of doing things and they clashed. The former GM engineer was used to basing a new automobile on what's called a master body draft. This sets the absolute external dimensions of the car and the mechanical

pieces are made to fit inside. When Collins pressed Chapman for a master body draft of the De Lorean, Chapman finally told him, "You don't understand how we build cars here." Lotus wanted to build the plastic underbody, find out how much it would shrink, then construct the body around the result.

Through all this, memos from Bill Collins to John De Lorean wondered at the amount of time it was taking to get the project underway. To make things even more awkward, De Lorean hired the highly respected engineer, Mike Loasby, from Aston Martin to a position Collins didn't really understand in relation to Collins' job.

It was all coming apart for Bill Collins. He felt as though he was being shuffled further to the sidelines, and it became increasingly obvious that the DMC-12 would end up the product of Colin Chapman's Lotus philosophy, not Bill Collins' De Lorean philosophy. So Collins resigned, said good-by to Kimberley and Rudd, and had a last dinner with Loasby to pass on any final information . . . and said to himself, "Good luck, it's your baby now."

On March 1, 1979, Bill Collins started work as the Director of Product Planning for American Motors in Detroit. Perhaps it was his time at De Lorean, or maybe it's just that engineers such as Collins are better off outside large companies, but two and one half years later, Collins left AMC to start Vixen Motor Co. with another former De Lorean employee, Bob Dewey, who had been De Lorean's first chief financial officer. They plan to build a new type of motor home, and returning full circle, Mike Pocobello of Triad is building their first prototype.

Although Collins had never totally agreed with the concept of having an outside firm do the final engineering of the DMC-12, he admits it could have worked. He now says of the decision to go to Lotus,

"I don't blame John for that, but I do blame him for not thinking about what it would do to me."

Lotus Total Technology

From the point of view of Lotus and its founder, Colin Chapman, their involvement with the De Lorean project was ideal. The Norwich, England-based low-volume automaker was trying to broaden its economic base and establish a division called Lotus Total Technology as an independent engineering and development company separate from Lotus' car-making function. Porsche—another company considered for development of the De Lorean—had done this very successfully, hiring their services out to other car manufacturers to help develop new automobiles. A project as large and well known as the De Lorean would add both money and, perhaps even more important, prestige to Lotus' research subsidiary.

Lotus was founded by Colin Chapman, who first used the name on an Austin 7-based special he built just after World War II while an engineering student at London University. Lotus Engineering was formed in 1952 and from the start was famous for little sports racing cars that were based on fairly common production parts, but that could often beat larger, much more expensive cars. Part of Chapman's secret was to keep his cars very light, a point some race drivers used to say made them overly fragile.

The line of Lotus race cars progressed from the lowly Mark 1 to the famous Mark 11 sports car; the company's first Grand Prix car, the Mark 12; and then a progression of other successful cars, all famous to racing enthusiasts merely by their numbers and including the 18, 23, the innovative monocoque 25, the 29 Indy car, 33, 49, and the Lotus 78, a pioneer ground-effects Grand Prix car in which Mario Andretti ultimately won the World Driving Champion in 1978, driving the perfected version, the Lotus 79.

From the sports racers of the late 1950s to ground effect Formula 1 Grand Prix cars of the last few years, Lotus has been a dominant force in racing and the cutting edge in new technology. Colin Chapman applied the same kind of thinking to his road cars, with his first, the beautiful 1960 Lotus Elite, pioneering much of what is now commonplace in automotive engineering.

Lotus Production History

Along with race cars came the Lotus cars built for the street, beginning in 1957 with the 7, which was really a race car with fenders. Next was the graceful Elite, sold from 1959 until 1963 and featuring an all-fiberglass unit body. Starting in 1962 and manufactured for 11 years was the smooth Elan, the first of the Lotus production cars based on a center steel backbone frame, the same concept used under the De Lorean. Lotus also added life to the rather common Ford Cortina sedan by installing the Lotus dual-overhead camshaft version of a Ford engine and creating another legend, the Lotus-Cortina. The Elan was stretched into the none-too-pretty Elan Plus 2, which lasted from 1967 to 1974. Lotus' first mid-engine production car, the Europa, was built between the years 1967 and 1975. In 1974, Lotus made the move up-market from these smaller sports cars when it introduced the new Elite, which was larger, still front-engined, powered by Lotus' own 2.2-liter 4-cylinder engine, based on a steel backbone frame and, like all production Lotuses except the 7, clothed in fiberglass. Another version of this car, the Eclat, was introduced in 1975, the same year as the lovely mid-engine Lotus Esprit. Like the De Lorean, the Esprit had an exterior design by Italian Giorgetto Giugiaro and both came from what one might call the designer's square-corner wedge period.

Lotus production cars have a reputation for being light, nimble, fast, a great deal of fun to drive, and able to make the most of a gallon of gasoline. Unfortunately, they are also known to be unreliable—with equal blame for this going to both the cars and the system for distributing and servicing them—and this has kept them from ever being a force in the U.S. market.

After a number of failed attempts to get sales started in America, Lotus signed an agreement with Rolls-Royce in 1980 that had Rolls marketing Lotus in the U.S. Despite, or perhaps because of, this agreement, Lotus virtually disappeared from the American market after that, with only the leftover cars being sold. In 1981 only 80 new Lotuses were registered in the States, so they were never going to be a threat to De Lorean, but it does raise the question of whether or not they were the ideal choice to do the engineering of John De Lorean's sports car. Looking back on it, John De Lorean feels they were, saying, ". . . I'm convinced we got a much less expensive job (at Lotus) and a much better job than in the States. Possibly Porsche could have done a better job, but it would have taken much more time." And extra time was one thing DMC didn't have.

What Did Lotus Have To Offer?

There were several things Lotus Total Technology could do for De Lorean. An example was demonstrated when they developed the Talbot Sunbeam Lotus. This began with a model called the Sunbeam that was something of a leftover when Peugeot bought Chrysler in Europe and changed the name of the cars to Talbot. A front-engine/rear-drive cousin of the Dodge Omni/Plymouth Horizon sold in the U.S., this Talbot model was sold with any of four engines with 42, 59, 69, 80 or 100 horsepower, but the car didn't have a particularly sparkling reputation. Lotus, on the other hand, had plenty of its 150-horsepower, 2.2-liter twin-cam 4-cylinder engines available now that the Jensen-Healey was dead. Under contract to Talbot, Lotus developed and remanufactured a version of the Sunbeam with the Lotus engine. The once-frumpy model went on to win the World Manufacturers Rally Championship in 1981.

It helped that Lotus and De Lorean were both small, specialist automakers, with neither having a large, cumbersome upper management group. The

Lotus engineer Colin Spooner deserves much of the credit for the chassis and suspension design of the De Lorean. Here he explains an idea to (from left) John De Lorean, Eugene Cafiero, Colin Chapman, and Mike Kimberley. (Howarth for Woodfin Camp & Associates)

men who needed to make top-level decisions could, at least in theory, get right to their counterparts at the other firm. Lotus also understood the needs, and limitations, of a small limited-production car maker, having been a low-volume auto producer since Colin Chapman first introduced his Elite.

Fiberglass technology was another advantage Lotus could offer De Lorean. The plastic inner body of the De Lorean sports car had been established from the beginning. Originally, of course, it was meant to be made by the Elastic Reservoir Molding (ERM) method being developed by another De Lorean company, Composite Technology Corporation, but now it was almost certain ERM wouldn't be used for the inner body. Whoever would develop the De Lorean would need experience in both automobiles and fiberglass. Several of Lotus Total Technology's projects had been based on plastics, from a set of furniture to parts for North Sea oil rigs, where the plastic could hold up against exceptionally bad weather.

Last and most important, Lotus offered the capability to finish the De Lorean project quickly. Time was running out, the contract with Northern Ireland was signed, the Giugiaro design was becoming too familiar and DMC's credibility was being stretched.

Of the original De Lorean crew, Zahutsky stayed on at Lotus for another 8 months after Collins quit. Emissions and safety expert Steve Matson remained for a total of 14 months, which he enjoyed, because, "I had no vested interest in any design package and I wasn't in any position to defend any concept that was developed." Mike Loasby, the respected and soft-spoken man who became the ranking De Lorean engineer when Collins left, describes the Collins/Chapman episode by saying, "Lotus had quite reasonably decided to design it [the De Lorean] their way, since they had the responsibility, which included a major rethink of the substructure."

As Lotus began to get into the De Lorean project, the DMC contingent at Hethel was headed by C. K. Bennington, an ex-Chrysler executive who was the main liaison between the two companies and shuttled back and forth between Hethel and Belfast. Loasby's official capacity was as the quality assurance man, a post that didn't reflect his talents.

Stand The Company On Its Head

The De Lorean effort was a relatively large one for Lotus, for which, Kimberley says, "We were prepared to stand our company on its head." At the time, Lotus employed about 450 men and women. They worked in a series of buildings constructed in a compound at the edge of a World War II airstrip. Across the road in a separate—and confidential—area is the Formula 1 team, which is an entirely different company. For the sort of automobiles Lotus builds the location is excellent. The roads leading from Norwich through farmlands to Hethel are narrow and twisty, often bounded with hedges or low berms. Quite simply, the men who drive to work each day at Lotus aren't about to design and build wide, heavy, ponderous automobiles.

For the De Lorean project, Lotus set aside 46,000 square feet of space for development work and another 20,000 square feet for administration offices, pattern shops, drawing offices, fabricating shops, an NVH (Noise, Vibration, Harshness) laboratory and the project's own road test and development center. About the only thing the De Lorean project shared with Lotus were the engine and emissions test cells. Most of the De Lorean space was in the World War II hangars near the factory, and those hangars had to be refurbished.

Heading the Lotus effort on the De Lorean was a design committee of four men. Naturally Colin Chapman was at its head, laying down the basic con-

Mike Loasby, who was Bill Collins successor, fits a scale model of the "backbone" chassis into a model of the VARI fiberglass underbody. They are upside down here, as in the actual car the underbody sits on top of the backbone. (Howarth for Woodfin Camp & Associates)

cepts he felt should be developed for the De Lorean. Kimberley, an ex-Jaguar engineer, was coordinator between Chapman's ideas and the men who made them into fiberglass and sheetmetal. Colin Spooner had the very important job of heading development of the De Lorean's chassis and body, while ex-BRM Grand Prix team designer Tony Rudd was in charge of getting the drivetrain ready.

Backed Into A Corner

Initially 180–190 Lotus employees were alotted or added-on for the De Lorean project, but first there was the time- and cost-consuming renovation of the hangars and other buildings to accommodate the people and shop equipment. Yet time had backed Lotus and De Lorean into several corners.

The entire De Lorean design project was meant to take 18 months, but that is the usual time required just to have body tools made before an automaker can begin stamping out body panels. There was no way for Lotus to completely engineer the DMC-12's chassis, drivetrain and underbody and *then* begin on the exterior body panels. The lack of time thus forced them to work *backwards*, establishing the final exterior *first* and then developing the car *inside* it. In retrospect, it is fair to say that there is probably no other automobile company around today which could have pulled it off. Certainly a Ford or GM has the resources, but they aren't light enough on their corporate feet to react and perform to such a tight schedule and unusual approach. Colin Chapman was used to re-engineering race cars in the transporter on the way to the track— and winning. This ability to work under pressure is a tradition at Lotus, and coupled with their extensive and advanced fiberglass know-how, enabled them to succeed where others would have failed.

For example, another time problem involved outside suppliers, who have a set lead time to begin delivering everything from window glass to headlight switches. This was particularly critical with an automobile such as the De Lorean, because it is basically an assembly of parts from outside sources, with few pieces actually manufactured in the Northern Ireland factory. And yet those outside suppliers need time to tool and begin production. Normally Lotus would have waited until after the design of the De Lorean was essentially complete before placing these orders. Instead, they had to initiate them as soon as the parts were decided on, at whatever point that was in the development of the car.

Kimberley admits that given their druthers Lotus would have scrapped the DMC-12's gullwing doors and stainless steel body and changed the design to make the car mid-engine instead of rear-engine. John De Lorean rejected those suggestions and Lotus, being an independent engineering firm, had no choice but to go ahead and work within the client's specifications. Nonetheless, the mark of Lotus was quick and deep on the De Lorean.

As Kimberley explains it, "I think one of the main reasons John De Lorean thought that Lotus would be appropriate for this job was that the time limit from start-up to having the car in production was, by normal car industry standards, incredibly short. On the other hand, we recommended, in principle anyway, the transfer of Esprit technology fundamentally, to insure that the shortest time possible was spent on engineering and development and all solutions from the engineering front could follow, as far as humanly predictable and practical, a right-first-time philosophy . . . and to short circuit a hell of a lot of learning curves."

Give It Some Backbone!

Outwardly there appeared to be only one major mechanical change between the second De Lorean

An excellent shot of the De Lorean's "backbone" chassis, showing the fuel tank tucked between the forks of the front "Y" with the radiator out front, and the engine placed similarly in the rear "Y". Compare this with the Lotus Elan chassis on the facing page. (DMC)

This is an ad for the 1965 Lotus Elan convertible, the first road car to use Colin Chapman's "backbone" chassis, in this case carrying the engine up front. By widening the center box-section just enough to fit in a driver, Chapman created the monocoque Formula 1 racing "tub," which still remains today's basic race car design.

prototype and the production version, but underneath was a complete redo. The two De Loreans thus far had been based on a plastic inner body, with the front suspension and steering attached to a front subframe, and the rear suspension and drivetrain bolted to a separate rear subframe. Lotus scrapped that design and installed their favorite chassis: a center backbone.

Considering that every Lotus production car since the Elan was introduced in 1962 has had a center backbone chassis, it isn't surprising that this same design feature was almost immediately incorporated into the De Lorean. Even Bill Collins, who admired the mid-engine Lotus Esprit and bought one as a test vehicle for the De Lorean company in 1975, had allowed for the possibility of a backbone when he did the original De Lorean design.

The principle of the backbone chassis is quite simple . . . which is one of its advantages. Think of it as a square-section steel beam that stretches from the front of the car to the rear and is the structural platform of the car. The front and rear suspensions become an outgrowth of the backbone, which also holds the steering, brakes wheel and radiator. The engine, whether placed at the front or rear, can be integral with the backbone. Like a spine, the center section is able to contain many of the important fore-aft connections, including a driveshaft if the car is front-engine, the plumbing to carry coolant from a

radiator to a rear engine, and the wiring harness. Mike Loasby adds, "In my view a backbone structure is beneficial in production terms because it holds both ends of the car together while you're building the chassis, and you get better alignment."

Swapping ERM for VARI

The next important change was replacing the ERM process in the De Lorean's manufacturing scheme. Lotus' ready-made replacement is called VARI (Vacuum Assisted Resin Injection). The ERM system would have split the inner body into upper and lower halves. These would have been stamped in dies as a fiberglass-foam-fiberglass sandwich, then the upper and lower halves joined to make one inner body. VARI stayed with the upper and lower halves part of it, gluing the two together to form one inner body, but the dies were replaced with molds. Sheets of fiberglass would be laid into the female side of a mold, a male side lowered into it, then clamped tight and sealed. The air in the mold would be evacuated to create a partial vacuum, assisting the flow of resin being pumped into the mold, where it would mix with the fiberglass to create half an inner body. Trading ERM for VARI meant dropping what promised to be an advanced process for a much more conventional but well known one.

Not incidentally, making the switch from ERM, for which he held the license, to VARI, which Colin Chapman owned, cost John De Lorean $5.1 million in further licensing fees.

The third and largest task Lotus had with the De Lorean was the detail development of the car. This meant establishing absolutely the length, width, breadth, shape, weight and strength of everything that would go into the De Lorean from the large sheetmetal panels to the smallest screw on the instrument panel. Eighteen prototype De Loreans—clothed in fiberglass

De Lorean front suspension is identical to Lotus Esprit: upper A-arm, single lower arm and anti-roll bar.

Rear suspension is Lotus Esprit philosophy adapted to larger, heavier car, with addition of upper link.

bodies instead of stainless steel because there were no panels and the styling was to be changed slightly— were built for development of the body and chassis. Of these, 10–11 spent hundreds of thousands of miles on the roads branching out from Hethel. A further 22 prototypes were constructed for various safety and crash tests, including air bag tests. Test rigs were built to check the durability of individual parts, from some that carried out multi-million cycles on torsion bars, to vibration rigs that gave the chassis and suspension such a pounding that they did 100,000 miles standing still in a few days.

An American Esprit

In Hethel, the De Lorean was, quite predictably, becoming more and more an American Lotus Esprit. Construction of the De Lorean underbody is very

LOTUS ESPRIT VS. DE LOREAN
A Comparison:

	Lotus Esprit		De Lorean
Wheelbase (in.)	96.0	...	94.8
Length (in.)........	167.7	...	168.0
Width (in.)........	73.2	...	78.3
Height (in.)	43.8	...	44.9
Curb weight (lb.) ...	2350	...	2840
Horsepower	140 @ 6500 rpm	...	130 @ 5500 rpm
Torque (lb.-ft.)	130 @ 5000 rpm	...	162 @ 2750 rpm

similar to that of the exterior of the Esprit, the fundamental difference being the stainless steel covering. There is the marked similarity with the center backbone chassis, though the De Lorean's is larger and stiffer, because the car is wider and heavier. The two cars' front suspensions are identical in description, with an

A fiberglass-bodied "mule," one of 18 such prototypes built by Lotus for testing, grinds out the miles on the test track at Hethel. (DMC)

DMC's Lotus Esprit. Bill Collins bought one of the mid-engined exotic cars early on for comparison purposes, not realizing then that the De Lorean Sports Car would wind up adopting most of its engineering technology. (Ludvigsen)

upper a-arm and a single lower suspension arm, while the anti-roll bar which is mounted ahead of the suspension is used to prevent front-to-rear movement of the lower arm. There are beefier pieces for the heavier De Lorean and the necessary design modifications to fit the suspension in the larger design "envelope" of the stainless steel car. The rear suspension is, again, the Esprit philosophy adapted to a larger, heavier car. There is an angled trailing arm to each wheel hub and a lower control link, but in the De Lorean there is also an upper link for better suspension control, while in the early Esprits the driveshaft was meant to double as an upper link. In the Turbo Esprits and, later, the Esprit S3, the mid-engine Lotuses were converted to the same system.

Even with the chance to adapt the Esprit philosophy to the De Lorean, the project was becoming something other than what Lotus had originally intended. Kimberley comments, "From the information we were given at the time (the 1978 trip to Phoenix) it looked as though it was a fairly straightforward case of taking the car and converting it into prototypes, crash testing and doing a development spec we could give back and say, 'Well, there's a car, you do the production engineering on it and away you go.' We'd been looked at to carry out what we'd call the mid-field development . . . design and development and initial prototype certifications, but not the final certification work. But then, later, the job grew."

That last comment of Kimberley's is an excellent example of classic British understatement, for in August, 1979, just as Lotus was really getting humming on the project, John De Lorean brought them a change that just about *did* stand the company on its head.

Just a Styling Tweak

Here's what happened: On the correct assumption that the styling of the DMC-12 was becoming

somewhat dated, De Lorean sent the original epo-wood styling mock-up back to Ital Design and had Giorgetto Giugiaro revamp the car's styling. Recall that in 1975 Giugiaro had done a series of design modifications with a black pen on Polaroid prints of the original epo-wood mock-up to demonstrate to De Lorean and Bill Collins how various window treatments would look on the DMC-12. The final choice then had been sketch Number 2, with the window cut below the car's "beltline" to provide somewhat better vision to the side. Now, in 1979, with the chance to redo the design of the De Lorean, Giugiaro reverted to his first choice, sketch Number 1, which has a continuous beltline from the hood to the bottom of the side windows and then to the bottom of the rear quarter windows. Also, the two individual vents between the two side windows were visually integrated into one.

No one would argue the changes didn't help update the De Lorean, Kimberley commenting that, "At the time the consensus of opinion was that the new, slightly softer, updated styling was a distinct improvement and made it into a car of the Eighties rather than a car of the late Seventies." Yet this "styling tweak," as De Lorean described it, changed the body envelope significantly for those trying to make all the pieces fit inside it, where thousandths of an inch are critical.

What Ital Design had actually redesigned was half the original epo-wood mock-up, putting the new lines to one side of this "car." That was all that was necessary for Lotus and when the mock-up was shipped to Hethel, Lotus took dimensional, 3-plane digital read-out figures on the new "half shape" and applied them to the entire automobile. These were transferred into large drawings and then detail drawings of the new exterior envelope. The trick then was to redo the plastic inner body to fit within the stainless steel skin. Lotus did a first set of tools for the inner

Here Colin Chapman, along with (from left) Eugene Cafiero, Mike Kimberly, Colin Spooner, John De Lorean and C.K. Bennington review styling variations provided by Giorgetto Giugiaro in the form of sketches made on Polaroids of the full-scale model (above and pages 98-99). Given opportunity to update his 1975 design, Giugiaro in August 1979 reverted to the side window treatment he had originally prefered (the #1 Polaroid). The styling "tweak" created severe problems at Lotus, forcing a myriad of small but critical adjustments. (Howarth for Woodfin Camp & Associates)

The full scale epo-wood model adjusted on one side by Giugiaro with the new side window treatment and single side vent. (DMC)

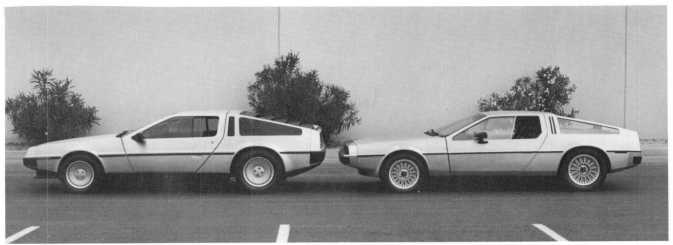

Comparison of original De Lorean prototype (right) with pre-production car (note sliding side window). Prototype's side window notches downward, production car has continuous straight line off the fender top. (Tony Hogg)

body, molded the body, measured the shrinkage in every dimension and plane of the body after it had cured, and then readjusted the master body draft to make another set of mold tools. Describing this task in one simple sentence belies the enormity of the job.

This was the pressure that turned Lotus on its head. The staff of the project was increased from the 180 level to 250–300, which is quite large considering the pre-De Lorean employment level of 450. They were rushing to meet the lead times of the various manufacturers who would supply all pieces of the De Lorean and none were more important, of course, than the stainless steel body panels.

Another Miracle

There was an even more immediate need for the panels than could possibly be met by the firms producing the final body panel dies. It had been 1977 when the first De Lorean prototype was shown at the National Automobile Dealers Association meeting in New Orleans in that first push for dealers. Credibility in the entire De Lorean project badly needed a boost, and to do that the company planned to show a final "production" DMC-12 to the dealers in the same room when the NADA returned to New Orleans in February, 1980. So, while Lotus was beavering away at the inner body, a set of the dimensions they had taken from the epo-wood mock-up was sent to a company in Detroit called Visioneering. Normally a company that makes stamping tools would require months to produce the dies from which an automobile's body panels are made. Somehow Visioneering took only six weeks to produce the Kirksite dies from which were stamped the first sets of panels for the Lotus/De Lorean prototypes . . . and made it possible to meet that NADA goal.

By December, 1979, Lotus had begun turning over some parts of the sports car to De Lorean, but development was by no means finished. There were still thousands of miles of emissions and fuel economy certification to run, Rudd and his crew eventually getting the latter from its original 18.6 mpg to 22.3 mpg on the U.S. Environmental Protection Agency's city cycle.

The size of the De Lorean staff at Lotus grew to as many as 25 when things really got hectic. Specifications from the prototype phase of the operation had to be transferred to production engineering as the factory was ready to start accepting the parts that would eventually lead to full production. The agreement with Lotus provided for the staff at De Lorean to be trained in making body-mold tools for the VARI inner body and those teams had to be trained at Hethel.

By the end of December, 1980, the De Lorean factory was only weeks away from producing its first car and the Lotus factory was finished with the project. The final six months at Hethel had seen the bulk of the work finally shifted to Belfast. Many of the workers who had come to Lotus for the De Lorean project had left and the large hangars were quiet.

5

Building The Factory

I T WAS TOUGH enough trying to get a new automobile ready for production, but the De Lorean Motor Company also needed a place to build it. Time was tight, threatening to outdate the sports car even as it was being developed at Lotus. If there wasn't a factory ready to start producing the car on time, all the investors, dealers, good intentions, and $110 million wouldn't mean a thing.

There was a great deal of snickering in the U.S. over the idea of De Lorean building his automobile factory in Northern Ireland. It didn't help when the project's critics heard that the site would be 72 acres in Dunmurray, just six miles from downtown Belfast and right between the Catholic district of Twinbrook and a Protestant area near Lisburn Road. Certainly a terrorist group would sneak in under cover of darkness and destroy the place. Even the English and Northern Irish governments recognized this possibility, allowing in their agreement for compensation should the factory ever be damaged by terrorists.

Fifty Percent Unemployment

What outside observers couldn't see, however, were the economic problems facing the local workers in that area of West Belfast. General unemployment was at 11 percent when the factory was started, though some put the Catholic rate at closer to 40–50 percent. Twinbrook was a particularly difficult area because its population was made up of Catholics who had been displaced from central Belfast by urban renewal, only to find there was housing, but few jobs, in the surrounding area. Welfare was becoming a way of life for many of the families there. Irish newspaper reports of the time didn't dwell on the problems that would come with mixing Catholic and Protestant workers, but on the advantages of an extra 2,000–2,500 incomes that would then help develop still more jobs in these suffering districts.

Many outsiders also didn't fully realize that Belfast has an industrial history of some note, with huge shipyards such as those of Harland and Wolff and the famous linen factories at the turn of the century . . . though the latter were often infamous for their atrocious working conditions.

Northern Ireland also has something of an automotive heritage. Robert Chambers and his brother, J.A., produced a series of highly regarded automobiles bearing the family name in Belfast between 1904 and 1925, though the firm finally succumbed to insufficient capital in 1929. J. B. Ferguson tried to build his Fergus automobiles—perhaps the first ever to use rubber engine mounts—in Belfast in 1915, but was hindered by World War I, eventually trying to produce the car in Newark, New Jersey. He tried again with a car called the O.D., but though both models were well designed, he failed again. Easily the most notable chapter in Belfast's automotive history was when John Boyd Dunlop developed an air-filled tire for his son's tricycle, beginning the modern pneumatic tire industry.

There's even automobile racing history in Ireland, the 1903 Gordon Bennett Cup race being held there when the proper host country, England, wouldn't allow racing on its roads. Legend has it the English racing color is green in honor of Ireland for saving the English motorists' honor and keeping the cup race in the British Isles. The Ards Circuit and the treacherous Dundrod race course were set up on public roads not far from the De Lorean factory, and a drive from Belfast's airport to the factory takes you along a small section of the Dundrod track. More recently, Grand Prix star John Watson is a Belfast native.

Work on the De Lorean factory began immediately after the contract was signed in late July, 1978. As it was later described, all they had were a picture of a car and a picture of a building. DMC Vice

Toasting the future at the ground breaking for the plant on October 2, 1982 are (L to R) Hon. Don Concannon (Northern Ireland's Minister of State), the De Loreans, and David Cook, Lord Mayor of Belfast. (DMC)

President, C. R. "Dick" Brown, who had gone to Belfast for the signing, returned to Northern Ireland almost immediately to start getting things settled at the factory site, hiring both men and companies to get the job done. Brown needed someone to help ramrod the construction of the building, so he called on the same man who had helped him at Mazda, Dixon Hollinshead of Costa Mesa, California . . . who ended up spending two years in Northern Ireland.

A Sodden Peat Bog

As Hollinshead explains it, when he got to Dunmurry, the site of the future De Lorean factory was only a pasture with cows grazing on it. And it was soggy land at that, purported by some to be a sodden peat bog that would require pilings to be dug before any building could be started. Luckily that proved untrue, but it was necessary to reroute two streams that once met on the property—which is in a natural

bowl—around the perimeter of the plot to meet on the far side. Hollinshead, Jerry Williamson and other early De Lorean workers also had to refurbish the only building on the site into an office building.

Despite this preliminary work, the De Lorean factory was officially started on October 2, 1978, with the ground breaking in the huge green field . . . though the ceremony had a certain air of foreboding. The weather wouldn't cooperate, providing an overcast, misty day. The plan was to have John De Lorean and Northern Irish dignitaries plant three trees to symbolize the involvement of De Lorean, England and Northern Ireland. There was even a brass plaque to be set among the trees.

All the necessary dignitaries—including the Honorable Don Concannon, Northern Ireland's Minister of State; Alderman David Cook, the Lord Mayor of Belfast; and Mrs. E. Kelsey, Her Worshipful the Mayor of Lisburn—and the press were assem-

bled near the one concrete block building that already existed on the site, when the protestors arrived. It was a group of Irish Republican Army supporters from Twinbrook, come to protest in sympathy with the political prisoners in Cell Block H, the section in which Bobby Sands lived before starving himself to death in early summer, 1981. The Catholic group had banners and placards and shouted "Murderers," "Killers," and other obsceneties. The ceremony had to be moved to the tent that had been set up in case of rain, but with open sides that was of little help.

Police protection had been provided, and Bill Collins remembers the group as being more noisy than threatening, but Williamson figures that, "If they'd had guns they would have shot at us." John De Lorean adds that, "They said they weren't protesting us, they were primarily protesting Don Concannon, who kept taunting them through the fence. I felt like hiding under a car, to be honest with you."

De Lorean says he was really more concerned for his wife, and Williamson comments that De Lorean seemed to shut the whole thing out of his world on that morning so important to the future of the De Lorean Motor Company. After the tree-planting, the group watched as a convoy of 14 earthmovers rumbled onto the property and began scraping away at the earth. Then the ceremony moved inside, away from the protestors, for the usual round of speeches about the future.

In Belfast there was pride in the fact that much of the design and building of the De Lorean factory was to be done by Irish firms. Though Renault had been consulted in the basic design of the factory and the assembly lines, the facility's architects—Brodie and Hawthorne—were from Belfast. Two local construction firms, Farrans and McLaughlin & Harvey, did the major work, with other nearby companies doing the sub-contracted details.

No Joking Matter

Naturally there were some minor construction problems. Hollinshead remembers a scruffy bush reputed to be a "faerie tree." "I don't know if you've ever read any of the Irish myths and things about that," said Hollinshead, "but it isn't a joke over there. We joked about the thorny bush for awhile and then we tried to get one of the crew to cut it down and they wouldn't do it. They'd give us the story about Murphy, who went to cut one down once and cut his leg off. Then I spread a rumor that there was a $100 bill buried under it, but I couldn't get any takers . . . and then one day it was gone and they all went about their business. I was accused of cutting it down, but I didn't like the publicity, because I figured somebody might blame me for it and get mad about it." When the problems of the De Lorean Motor Company deepened in the spring of 1982, there were critics ready to resurrect the dangers of cutting down a faerie tree.

Although there was initial concern about the religious make-up of the work crews, nothing materialized, and the men went about the considerable work which had to be done. After scraping off the top layer of muck, the builders had to bring in over a million tons of rock from the hills behind the factory. They covered the entire factory site with two feet of this rock before they were ready to begin laying concrete for the factory foundations.

The plan was to have steel in the air by June 1, and they did, though later, as they were about to put up the body press building a major steel company went bankrupt, causing the other builders to carry on without an overhead structure, even putting in toilets and offices. Still later, after Lotus had taken over the development of the De Lorean, the switch from the ERM to the VARI process caused minor problems.

Nonetheless, progress on the De Lorean facility was impressive. With the exception of the fiberglass

(OPPOSITE): While the three trees symbolizing cooperation between England, Northern Ireland and De Lorean are planted with engraved shovels, IRA supporters are visible in the background protesting for the men imprisoned in Cell Block H, where Bobby Sands would starve himself to death in 1981. By then the empty field was four new buildings with over 500,000 sq. ft. An existing building of 50,000 sq. ft. (top center) was converted into administrative offices. (DMC)

(ABOVE) Ex-GM executive George Broomfield (left) played a critical role getting plant ready. Security chief Myron Stylianides is at right. (LEFT) Note half-mile test track at far left. Administrative offices are in lower right hand corner. (DMC)

underbodies there would be no actual manufacturing at the De Lorean factory, just assembly, so the company was saved some of the problems and costs involved in a total factory. Lotus began delivering some parts in December, 1979, and the tooling and the sourcing of parts was already underway, because these had to be ready when the factory was finished. Quiz the men involved and they'll tell you one of the great unsung heroes in getting the plant going was George Broomfield. An ex-General Motors executive who had worked for GM in manufacturing and production in Brazil, Argentina and West Germany, Broomfield was De Lorean Motor Company Limited's Director of Manufacturing, which meant he was responsible to make certain all the car's pieces were done properly, ready to go on the assembly line and then correctly

put together. The man in charge of buying all the necessary pieces was a former Reliant Motor Company director named Barry Wills.

Ready To Go

Only two years after the ground breaking, the De Lorean factory was ready to start running pre-production cars down the line to test the assembly methods, and the workers. This minor miracle of construction, having been finished in about half the time anticipated by many outside observers, was never completely appreciated.

"You have to remember," comments John De Lorean, "that when Ford built their plant in Valencia, Spain, they had 400 people from other places in the world who were assigned to that project—from

81

First production car rolled out January 21, 1981, but the next two months were spent practicing, as shown here. There were several hundred cars built for learning purposes by the brand new work force without any exterior stainless steel panels. After these so-called "black cars," production of shipable cars began in April, with chassis numbers starting at 500. (DMC)

Dearborn, from Germany, from England—and so they had a total cadre of competent management, production engineers, plant engineers, the whole thing. As a new little nickle-shit company we didn't have all those things, so it was much more difficult for us than it would be for other people."

One of the original studies for the proposed factory in Puerto Rico had suggested a single 500,000-square-foot building for De Lorean. Once in Northern Ireland, however, it was considered prudent—centered between Protestant and Catholic areas—to spread the things that needed to be done throughout several buildings for security reasons. It was more expensive this way, but the risks were evened out.

The De Lorean factory is made up of four buildings: the 205,000-square-foot Body Press Building in which the fiberglass underbodies were made, an Assembly Building of 272,000 square feet, a Fabrication and Storage Building measuring 50,000 square feet and a like-size Emissions and Vehicle Preparation Building. Most automobile factories—particularly outside the U.S.—are notable for (1) the amount of noise that assaults you from the moment you walk into the place, (2) smells that you suspect hint of things you shouldn't be breathing in, (3) a seeming waste of motion and energy, or (4) any combination of the preceding three. Being mainly an assembly area for parts bought from outside the company, and not a manufacturing plant, the De Lorean factory escaped the great majority of this nastiness.

The building that had been on the land from the start of the project was converted into administrative offices, and contained another 50,000 square feet. Tucked over in one corner of the property was a very neat 1/2-mile test track, complete with a steeply banked turn. There was even room to expand . . . when and if. . . .

Now that there was a De Lorean factory there were workers to be trained. Alan Watson, Jr., who reported the De Lorean story for the *Belfast Telegraph,* says, "The work force was extremely enthusiastic. A lot of the early workers were the sort of guys who were amateur auto enthusiasts, who had their own sports cars. They were men who wanted to be in on the development of a car from the early stages. We never had cars built in Northern Ireland, so it was quite a chance. . . ."

John De Lorean says of the workers in Northern Ireland, ". . . the people were wonderful, they're highly motivated, they work, they have industry, they're intelligent, [were] relatively easily trained . . . I think they became a very competent work force in a reasonable amount of time."

First Production Car: Jan. 21, 1981

There were the initial glitches expected in any project as large and as hurried as this. The gullwing doors had to have their own special assembly line, for instance, but on January 21, 1981, the first real production De Lorean rolled out of the building. Then it was a matter of the workers and managers and the car getting to know each other, so the process could be smoothed out.

There were several hundred cars, or at least inner body/chassis cars without the stainless steel, built initially. These were known to some as the "black cars" and were built for learning purposes. Actual production figures start at 500 and these cars, built in April and later, were the first De Loreans shipped to the U.S., arriving in June.

Eventually the expected trouble happened. On May 5, 1981, after the death of the first hunger striker, Bobby Sands, a small group of rioters got close enough to the factory to fire bomb a small wooden building. Unfortunately it contained the office of the company's

The first production cars to reach the U.S. were air-freighted in, arriving in New York in June. (DMC)

Chief Engineer, Mike Loasby, and many of the engineering drawings went up, so Loasby and crew had to collect a complete set from other offices and from suppliers. DMC applied for compensation from the Irish government, with a claim of $957,000. The government made a first payment of $372,000 against the claim on May 11, with further money being passed to DMC in June, August and October, for a total of $791,000. After the last payment, however, De Lorean pressed another claim that brought the total to $19.5 million because of drawings and records that were in the building at the time of the fire, and unduplicated elsewhere. This second claim was filed January 2, 1982, but rejected by the British.

During the "Troubles" in Belfast there were days when some workers would be gone to the funerals of the hunger strikers, and absenteeism would rise. There were other occasions when some workers would stop for periods of 15–20 minutes of silence to honor the hunger strikers. There were a few bomb threats that required evacuating the buildings. However, the single act of violence noted was the only one that marred the location's reputation. The company had let it be known that it didn't want to be involved in any sectarian disputes and that's about where it ended.

John De Lorean says his wife was concerned about his travel in Northern Ireland, considering De Lorean's position. He claims he received threats against himself, but adds that, "My theory of life is that if you're a target of a terrorist group there's really nothing you can do about it. If they can kill Lord Mountbatten, who had security beyond anything I could conceive of or afford, then I would have no shot [no pun intended, I suspect—Ed.] anyhow, so I have really never given it any thought."

Climbing The Quality Curve

As one might expect, the early cars off the

These underbodies were used for the practice assembly period in February/March 1981 when the workers were being trained. (DMC)

De Lorean assembly line required some corrections after they got to the States. The early examples needed as much as 140–200 hours of work on them at the company's two Quality Assurance Centers—in Bridgewater, N.J., and Santa Ana, Calif.—which at that point were very aptly named. Eventually, 30 De Lorean workers from Belfast were sent to De Lorean's California center to learn what the quality control problems were and how to solve them.

The proof of the success of the continuing quality control programs was seen in early 1982 when Gene Daly and Andy Weiss began their branches of the De Lorean Motor Car Club in California. An informal survey of the De Lorean owners showed that,

The assembly line swiftly moved up to 40 cars per week, and by July the proud and enthusiastic workers posed at the Belfast docks as car number 1000 was put on the boat for American enthusiasts. (DMC)

generally speaking, the higher the serial number of your De Lorean, the fewer the problems. Some critics of John De Lorean would add that the exception to this rise in the learning curve came in late November when he doubled the production rate at the factory from 40 cars per day to 80 and the quality slipped as the cars were moved down the line at this higher speed. Considering what those extra 40 cars per day did to jam up the distribution system and eat away the company's export financing, that day in November may go down as the beginning of the end of the De Lorean.

Add up the speed with which the De Lorean factory was built and the efforts made to assure that the cars coming out the far end of it were solidly built and no matter what happens to DMC in the end, one cannot pin any blame on the factory and the men who worked in it.

Needed: One More Miracle

Now, of course, the Body Press and Assembly Buildings are empty. The compact test track won't be used to check any more just-assembled De Loreans. The minor miracle it took just to get the factory up and running in such a short time is nothing compared to the miracle it will take to get the place into operation again building De Loreans. And in all the press that accompanied the arrest of John De Lorean and the failure of his company, the honest accomplishment of the men who got the factory built and operating was again left out. Even that is nothing to what has happened to the workers.

In the end John De Lorean's "dream" was just a bad dream for the workers in the De Lorean factory. The closing of the factory was more than a loss of a job to many of the men and women who had worked there. They had shown they were made of better stuff than their critics would have one believe, and now they have nothing to show for it. Alan

Watson of the *Belfast Telegraph* explains: "Of all the people who had to depend on De Lorean, it was the people who lived near the factory, especially in the Catholic part of West Belfast called Twinbrook, who stood to lose the most. There's very little work for them to do and it never has been an area with a great deal of industrial experience. A lot of the people who live there work in service industries, they work in hotels and pubs, and they certainly had no experience with automobile assembly, so they went into it not knowing what to expect. They got a good wage, they got training, somebody paid attention to them for a change and wanted to help them carve out some sort of career, so they of all people had the most to lose . . . and they of all people lost the most.

"If you balance that against £80 million with the British government, 80 million is a drop in the ocean in total government expenditures. But for those people, when De Lorean goes down the tubes then they have nothing left. Not only have they lost their hope, but they've lost hope of finding alternative employment. The sort of company that employs 2,000 people nowadays is rare in Northern Ireland."

In the beginning one of the biggest question marks hanging over the De Lorean project was the choice of Northern Ireland as a factory site, and in the apparent ending the workers and the factory are probably the most valuable asset which remains. But in all the fuss over John De Lorean's problems the minor miracle caught between Twinbrook and Lisburn is slipping under the waves, a ghostly echo of the brave Titanic, constructed by Belfast workers not so many years ago. If you remember, the Captain ordered full speed ahead through the calm and moonlit North Atlantic that night of April 14, 1912, shortly before the iceberg mortally sliced the ship open. Captain Edward J. Smith went down with the ship, along with 1503 hapless souls stranded without lifeboats.

Ghostly echo of the De Lorean's loss, SS Titanic heads out Belfast Lough for sea trials in 1912. (BBC Hulton Library)

6

"Star Wars" Assembly Line

T HERE WAS SOMETHING on the order of $110 million already spent by the De Lorean Motor Co. when its first sports car began to inch its way down the Dunmurray assembly line in January, 1981. John De Lorean and C. R. Brown had accomplished the small miracle of having raised the money to build the automobile. A cadre of very hard-working men had then gotten the factory built in an amazingly short time. Lotus had developed the car in quick order. But it would all mean nothing if the De Lorean Sports Car couldn't be assembled economically and reliably.

This was the stuff of fascination for those watching and ulcers for the executives on the inside. Although assembly line workers are generally classed by the bean-counters as "unskilled," that word is the antithesis of what their bosses at De Lorean expected of them. There was $110 million on the line—they *had* to get it right. Fortunately, though there has been a great deal of unemployment and civil strife in Belfast, the city has a history testifying to real industrial skill on the part of the work force. The local shipyards— now in a depressed state—were once the best in the world. When the *Titanic* was launched in Belfast in 1912 it was the most technically advanced passenger ship on the seas.

Manufacturing A De Lorean

The construction of a De Lorean began in the tall single-story Body Press Building, where the plastic underbodies were made. These internal structures of the De Loreans have two halves which were made of fiberglass in molds that were built and maintained in the De Lorean factory. Female molds for the upper and lower halves of the underbody began their slow, creeping journey through the building by having sheets of fiberglass made in France by Vetrotex Saint-Gobain hand-laid on their surface. At the same time, small

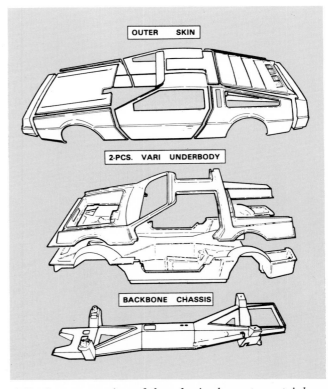

A De Lorean consists of three basic elements: a stainless steel skin, which attaches to a 2-piece fiberglass body which mounts atop a steel "backbone" chassis. (DMC)

beams made of foam were placed in certain areas of the shell that would have to take more stress in the finished body. A male mold was then lowered into the female mold, an overlapping lip around the pair sealed and air drawn out of the mold. This vacuum had two purposes, one to help close the molds together, the other to promote the flow of plastic resin to be injected in the next step.

The resin was added in three places in the mold,

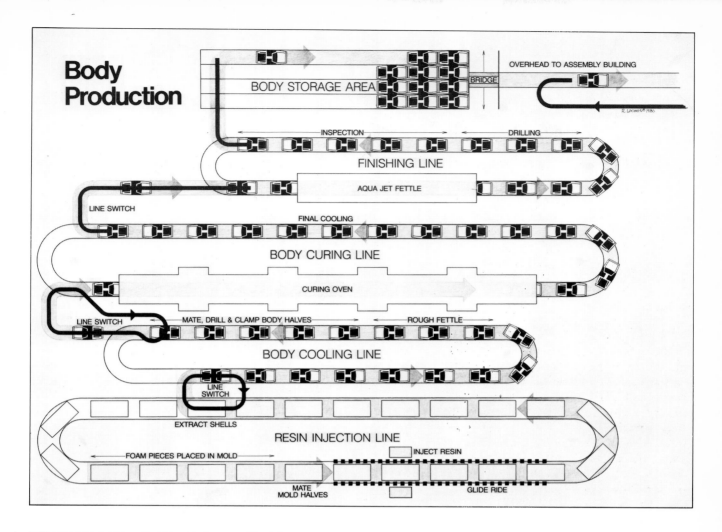

Body Production

R. Loomis © 1980

OVERHEAD TO ASSEMBLY BUILDING

BODY STORAGE AREA — BRIDGE

INSPECTION — DRILLING

FINISHING LINE

AQUA JET FETTLE

LINE SWITCH

FINAL COOLING

BODY CURING LINE

CURING OVEN

LINE SWITCH — MATE, DRILL & CLAMP BODY HALVES — ROUGH FETTLE

BODY COOLING LINE

LINE SWITCH

EXTRACT SHELLS

RESIN INJECTION LINE

FOAM PIECES PLACED IN MOLD — INJECT RESIN

MATE MOLD HALVES — GLIDE RIDE

(ABOVE) The production of the underbody, turning rolls of fiberglass and barrels of resin into cured, "fettled" shells. (DMC) (LEFT) Workers lift an underbody lower half from a female mold, after which it will be cooled, then joined with an upper half to create a full body. (DMC)

taking about six minutes to do so, and then the mold began a slow, smooth "Glide Ride." At Lotus this VARI process is allowed an initial setup time by merely letting the mold stay where it is for a short time. On the faster-moving De Lorean production line there wasn't this luxury of time and so the Glide Ride gently carried molds along their route. About 14 minutes into the 70-minute curing time, air was injected between the male mold and the curing body half to pop the

mold a bit and prevent the body from shrinking and sticking to the male mold. (The inside of the mold was also polished and coated with a release agent to prevent the fiberglass from sticking.) When the curing time was up, the new fiberglass upper (or lower) body was pulled from its mold, but more curing time was required before it could be worked on.

Soon, however, the process of cutting the windows and other necessary holes in the upper body half—a job known in England by the wonderful name "fettling"—was being done with routers and other high-speed cutting tools.

Gluing The Halves Together

Anyone who has ever built a plastic model car, boat or airplane would appreciate the next step, as the

A complete De Lorean underbody begins its trip through the curing oven where it will reach temperatures of over 200 degrees. (DMC) (FAR RIGHT) An underbody is lowered onto the chassis trim line, where everything from wiring to window glass will be added. (DMC)

two inner body halves were glued together. However there were no little tubes of glue, but great nozzles that oozed Goodyear Pliogrip adhesive onto the flanges of the two halves, which were then stapled to clamp the pieces together. The glue-setting process, a step that smaller fiberglass users would handle merely by letting the new piece sit until solid, was speeded up by De Lorean as the glued innerbody was slowly shuffled into a long oven. During the next 1-1/2 hours the body went through ever increasing heat, working in four stages from just over 100 degrees Fahrenheit to around 212 degrees.

Once cooled, the innerbody could go through its final fettling, including some cutting done with 60,000-pounds-per-square-inch water jets, a process that was particularly important around the holes which would become the gullwing door openings, because a proper seal here is more critical than in conventional doors. Also, master guide holes were drilled to locate a variety of jigs which align other pieces of the car as they are bolted on. Then a few extra fiberglass panels approximating the final external shape of the car—and the surface to which the stainless steel panels would be attached—were glued to the underbody. A final inspection, and some 13 hours after the molds first began their slow march along the assembly line there was one more complete De Lorean underbody. It was then attached to a conveyor belt which lifted it up and away to the Assembly Building.

Building The Underbody: Expensive

Lotus' hand in developing the De Lorean was very obvious in the process of building the underbody, because the Lotus Esprit body follows many of the same steps. At Hethel upper and lower body halves are laid up and then glued together with a seam that runs around the middle of the automobile. The major difference, of course, is that the stainless steel body panels are attached to the underbody of a De Lorean, while with the Esprit the fiberglass is the body and is accordingly painted and finished.

(Former De Lorean Motor Cars of America president, C. R. "Dick" Brown, comments that the adaptation of Lotus production techniques to the De Lorean added to the cost of the car. "Lotus designed the car to be a car, but they didn't design the car to be assembled. The objective was 50 manhours of assembly time per car and it happened to be 140. You've got three times the labor involved than was anticipated.")

The fiberglass underbody was only one of thousands of parts that went into the construction of a De Lorean, but it was one of the few actually manufactured at the factory. The mild steel backbone frames were welded up in England by the well-known company GKN. That same firm also supplied such parts as the constant velocity joints, some suspension stampings and, from their Kent Alloys Division, the aluminum alloy wheels. Additional suspension parts were made in England by Tallen Engineering, the anti-roll bar and springs provided by Jonas Woodhead & Sons Ltd. Disc brakes arrived from Lucas Girling, NCT tires from Goodyear, seats from Britax in England, the seat cushions from Vita Cortex, Ltd, and the leather used to cover them from Bridge of Weir Leather Co., Renfrewshire, Scotland. The car's window glass came from Saint-Gobain in France. Steering wheels were supplied by TRW Clifford in England.

From the U.S. came Sylvania headlamps, Tennaco Walker exhaust systems, interior hardware from Rockwell International, and some parts from divisions of General Motors: AC Spark Plugs provided the plugs and instrument cluster, Saginaw Steering Gear added the steering column, Harrison Radiator did the air conditioning evaporator and Delco Remy the battery. The plastic gas tanks were provided by

The Renault V-6 engine and transmission, which were shipped from France, are now prepared for the De Lorean, with all the specific pieces needed for installation into the rear-engine sports car being added. Quite a few women were employed on the assembly line. (DMC)

Dyno Industrier AS of Oslo, Norway. Parts for the gullwing doors included outside rearview mirrors made by Harman International Industries Gmbh in Germany, the torsion bars from Unbrako and the weatherstripping from Schlegel Corp. Engines and transmissions were shipped from the Peugeot-Renault-Volvo factory in Douvrain, France, the company's proper name being Societe Franco-Suedoise de Moteurs. And then there was that terribly important element of the De Lorean, the stainless steel body panels, stamped by Lapple (FRG) in West Germany from sheets that were cut and brushed by BSC Stainless of Sheffield, England.

As the list of the parts shows, the De Lorean was not a conglomeration of suspect parts gathered from fly-by-night companies. The men who designed the car were used to working with the top suppliers in the world and they continued to do so with DMC.

Upside Down Chassis Assembly

Both chassis and inner body begin their slow trips down the assembly line in different places. The chassis was still just the simple frame, looking spread eagle and bare, having just been picked from a pile of frames. These begin their build-up or "dressing" process by being turned upside down. This made it easier to add several of the parts that needed to go on first, such as the plastic fuel tank that is tucked within the forward "Y" of the frame, and the piping that carries coolant from the radiator back to the engine. After these first steps the frame was turned right-side up and began to inch its way through the remainder of the 17 stations on the chassis assembly line. Now the front and rear suspensions were added as was the radiator, additional bits of piping and a small maze of necessary lines and cables. The entire process was made easier because each of the frames was mounted on a carrier that elevated it so the workers could operate without

Completed De Lorean chassis is mounted on a 14-foot long Tellus carrier, which is driven by an electric motor and automatically follows a signal from a cable in the floor, moving from station to station. (DMC)

a great deal of bending or, in the case of assembly lines in which the chassis passes over a long pit in the floor, constantly reaching over their heads. Bit by piece the De Lorean went together.

The engine/transmission units shipped from France were not quite ready to be installed as received. They had to be prepped with the correct accessory drives and all the right plumbing pieces to allow the engine to be easily mounted in the rear "Y" of the frame and match all the tubes and wires . . . a job that involved nine different stations in a separate mini-assembly line. The transmissions were modified in the factory at Douvrain to run "backwards" from their usual position in the Renault 30 in which the engine

Originally, the gullwing doors were to be assembled on the same line as the cars, but after it was determined their build-time was higher, they got their own mini-assembly line. (DMC)

This diagram of the initial production line arrangement shows how the bare frames enter the chassis trim line (bottom), meet the engine line and, after completion, are mounted on a Tellus carrier. After the body and chassis are mated, the car goes to final assembly for its stainless steel panels. (DMC)

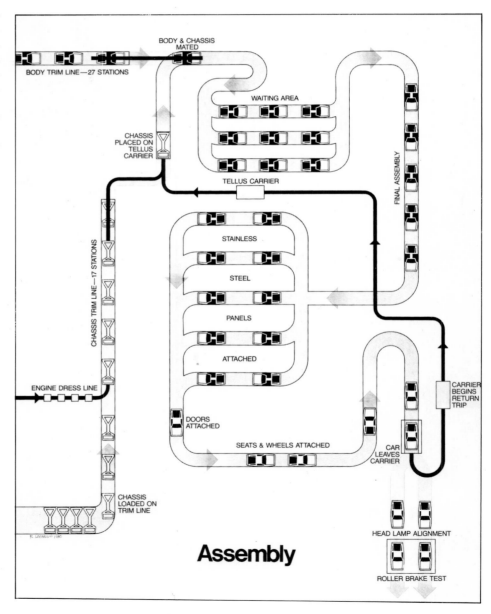

BODY TRIM LINE—27 STATIONS

BODY & CHASSIS MATED

WAITING AREA

CHASSIS PLACED ON TELLUS CARRIER

TELLUS CARRIER

FINAL ASSEMBLY

CHASSIS TRIM LINE—17 STATIONS

STAINLESS

STEEL

PANELS

ATTACHED

ENGINE DRESS LINE

CARRIER BEGINS RETURN TRIP

DOORS ATTACHED

SEATS & WHEELS ATTACHED

CAR LEAVES CARRIER

CHASSIS LOADED ON TRIM LINE

HEAD LAMP ALIGNMENT

ROLLER BRAKE TEST

Assembly

90

is ahead of the gearbox. Now all that was left was for each engine to be mated to a transmission before they were sent off their little branch of the assembly line and into a frame.

As the frames crept down their flush floor-mounted carriers, the underbodies were also moving slowly down their own line, this one with 27 stations. As with the frames, the bodies were elevated so the workers rarely had to bend more than halfway over, usually working at a very comfortable height. There were hundreds of pieces that had to be added here too, one important item being the car's electrical wiring. In the early cars this was quite a jumble because of the manner in which the electrical system "grew" as different components were designed into the car. This caused problems for initial buyers and was only really solved when the entire system was reworked and simplified, leaving 17 pounds of wiring on the cutting room floor. Also added at this point in production were such things as gullwing door hinges and striker plate bases, more tubes and cables, the ducting for the heating/air conditioning system . . . and on and on.

Orchestrating The Gullwing Door Assembly

At the same time, the gullwing doors were on their own mini assembly line, the complexity and importance of these large fixtures leading to their special treatment, and the need for 18 different steps in building a door. After production began it was found the cycle time to properly complete a set of doors didn't match the timing on the production lines and so they were built off to one side. It's difficult to believe how complex the inner workings of those doors are until you've seen one under construction, putting in the electric motors for the windows, the mechanism for the door latches and locks and ducting for the in-door vent. As in the other assembly lines there were frequent quality control checks of the doors. Because they were

On the body trim line (top photos) such pieces as window glass were added. The car is at waist level and workers don't have to reach or stoop. (DMC) (ABOVE) A trimmed De Lorean body being lowered on a completed chassis. (DMC)

such an important part of the De Lorean "dream" they had better be right . . . or the entire operation could become a nightmare. Ask someone who has been locked in his De Lorean.

After they were individually as complete as possible, the frame and underbody were now finally brought together at a junction of the two assembly lines. It looked deceivingly simple as the plastic part was lowered down on the completed chassis and bolted at the 10 body mounts, until one saw all the various connecting tubes and wires that now had to be joined.

At this point the body/chassis was mounted on a Tellus carrier. This is a lesson from the Swedes, who, because of their socialist system, have spent years and hundreds of manhours developing ways to improve the quality of life for their virtually un-fireable workers. The battery-powered Tellus carriers took the De Lorean from station to station controlled by a

Tellus carriers automatically move the De Loreans to the next station for their stainless steel skins. (DMC)

Almost finished, a De Lorean gets its wheels and will soon be lifted off the Tellus carrier. (DMC)

master computer that knew how much time the carrier needed at each stop. However, a worker could halt the carrier if there wasn't enough time to complete the work at his station. Silently the Tellus carriers followed metal lines buried in the floor in a rather spooky *Star Wars* manner with no apparent outside help, workers occasionally plugging into the carriers with a remote device that allowed direct control.

As the assembly line was first devised, the underbody would next have received its outer covering of stainless steel sheetmetal, but it was found to be very difficult to then make the doors fit the resulting opening. The assembly line was therefore revised so that once the various connections were made between body and chassis the car was guided into the gullwing door-mounting station. This was as difficult a process as building the doors—and just as critical considering the doors' importance, because a De Lorean with gullwing doors that don't close and fit correctly would be like an expensive suit which never quite fits to your satisfaction. In the early cars the use of doors built with temporary "soft" dies drove everyone slightly crazy as workers tried to make them fit correctly; however, this problem was basically solved with the arrival of the regular production doors. Still, the gullwings were never simply bolted on, but required some craftsmanship to make certain they closed easily and evenly

around the complex door seal.

Looking strangely naked with doors in place but no covering sheetmetal, the De Lorean now made its way to the next area, where the Tellus carriers automatically glided to the first empty station. At last the stainless steel could be bolted on. Because the sheetmetal was not part of the structure—and, in fact, was designed to be easily detachable for repair purposes—it could be attached directly to the fiberglass with no need for any strengthening under the glass. After the panels were carefully positioned and attached, the car was moved to the station at which the plastic front and rear caps with the head- and taillights were added . . . another early production line problem that had to be corrected to get the caps smooth and even with the bodywork.

A Shower Before Leaving

Now all a De Lorean needed were seats and wheels, which it got in the next station, along with a final electrical check, headlight adjustment, a slug of fuel and a lift off its Tellus carrier. The fuel was for an 8-minute engine test on a set of rollers to make certain everything was bolted together correctly and the engine was running properly.

After a new De Lorean left the factory the first thing it got was a shower. This soaking came from a set of high-pressure heads and was a check for water leaks. Before the car was shipped, temporary styrofoam pieces were added at each of its corners, front and back and on the sides to prevent minor damage on the docks or during shipping.

Then the De Loreans were loaded on car carriers for the short journey to the Belfast harbor . . . in what was hoped to be a long succession of car carriers. This wasn't to be, of course, and after some 8,000 De Loreans had been built, the *Star Wars* assembly line stopped, probably never to run again.

(ABOVE) An almost-completed De Lorean on a Tellus carrier during the period when the production line techniques were being finalized. (DMC) (LEFT) The final result of all the years of raising money and developing the car—the first De Loreans shipped to the U.S. by boat are unloaded in Long Beach, California. (DMC)

7

What John Hath Wrought

WHEN JOHN DE LOREAN, Bill Collins, Mike Pocobello, Colin Chapman, Mike Kimberley, Colin Spooner, Giorgetto Giugiaro, Tony Rudd, Mike Loasby—to name only the major characters in the story—had finally finished with the De Lorean Sports Car, the automobile had outwardly changed very little despite its five-year gestation period. The DMC-12 designation may have been dropped in favor of Sports Car, the exterior styling was slightly different, and it may not have been a safety car anymore, but the basic Giugiaro lines, stainless steel finish and gullwing doors meant the original character of the De Lorean remained intact.

Some of the car's critics felt too much of the original project was unchanged, in particular the De Lorean's styling. Giugiaro, who naturally has some interest in the success of the car, comments on the time delay by saying, ''Usually a project has to be ready

Giugiaro's initial styling changed only slightly in the five years it took to bring the De Lorean Sports car to production. Top: the 1975 plaster model. Middle: the first prototype (1978). Bottom: the final 1979 epowood model. (Ital Design) Below is the finished production car as shown in a foldout from the De Lorean sales brochure.

in four years. As it waits longer to enter the market it becomes more and more risky. Luckily, the De Lorean, being a classic car, can afford this delay without too much damage. Anyway, I feel the success of a sport or 'granturismo' car depends chiefly on its chassis.'' (Which statement either makes Giugiaro the most modest stylist of all time or the most tactful.)

Strother MacMinn, who for years has been an

DE LOREAN—the man, the company, the car

After 25 years of spectacular personal accomplishment in the automotive industry, John Z. De Lorean was convinced that it was possible to build a car with a useful life of more than just a few years. A total performance car that would be economical to run and safe to drive, without compromising quality and comfort for price. With the founding of the De Lorean Motor Company in 1975, he set out to prove it could be done.

It was an ambitious project, and only experts were called to the task. Top engineers and designers rendered the De Lorean concept with vision and foresight using corrosion resistant materials and new technology, and in just a few short years the dream began to take shape.

There is a new car on the road today. A car built with great care and commitment; a car that defies convention and challenges the future. The long-awaited transportation revolution has now begun, and a leader has emerged to show us the way . . . the 1981 De Lorean.

DE LOREAN—the next generation

The De Lorean sparks the imagination like a classic vision of things to come. New materials, new technology and traditional values masterfully joined in a showcase of contemporary engineering. Its precisely counterbalanced gull-wing doors rise on cryogenically preset torsion bars and need only 14 inches of side clearance. The softly brushed stainless steel exterior cannot fade or chip. Even the sporty rear louvers have been carefully designed to minimize aerodynamic drag, while they reduce window glare. Because you simply cannot create a masterpiece with arbitrary lines . . .

DE LOREAN—distinctive looks from any direction

The clean, uncluttered lines of the De Lorean's elegant low profile bear the unmistakable touch of true classic styling. Complimentary protective side trim runs the full length of the automobile; halogen headlights, side markers and high intensity backup lights provide maximum visibility and safety while driving after dark. Even the semi-rigid bumpers have been endowed with a "memory" which helps them return to their proper shape after a minor mishap. All of these, and more, are only part of De Lorean Motor Company's serious commitment to total driver satisfaction.

A stunning full color 16-page sales brochure was produced for the De Lorean Sports Car and is reproduced in its entirety above and on the next three pages. The only other sales literature was a small folder.

instructor and consultant on the subject of automotive design, says of the De Lorean, "It will remain contemporary because its proportions go beyond fashion . . . it is sufficiently individual even among specialist cars that it will retain its appeal for the general audience."

What's truly important about the De Lorean shape, as it leaves the factory, is, of course, the 304 alloy stainless steel that takes the form of the Giugiaro shape.

The Romance Of Stainless Steel

Giugiaro liked the idea of the stainless, commenting that because of this material the shape needed "to be clean, with flat surfaces, neat edges, etc., in order to emphasize and follow the material characteristics." The designer also approved of the idea of the cars all being the same color: "I love the monocolor because it emphasizes the shape rather than the 'chromatic game.' The stainless steel is a rather pure material. Without it the car wouldn't have its novelty and personality look."

Stainless steel also fit nicely into De Lorean's plan for an "ethical car." The fact that stainless won't rust made it an ideal material, particularly when you add in the fiberglass underbody and the epoxy-covered frame, both of which are also meant to last well beyond the usual life of an automobile. A plan to one day begin making the *frames* of stainless steel was still being considered after the start of De Lorean production.

The sales brochure measured 8 1/2" by 12", and featured two 24-inch foldouts along with some very handsome photography.

And if the company had succeeded, the next De Lorean, a 4-passenger sedan, was also to be clothed in stainless.

The discovery of stainless steels happened at the beginning of this century in Europe. Their commercial development came just before World War I. Considered iron-based alloys, stainless steels are usually best known for their resistance to corrosion. They have this quality because stainless steels have what is known as surface passivity, and while there are several theories as to just what causes this, the most common view is that a thin oxide film on the surface of the metal prevents the corrosion. It's the presence of at least 12 percent chromium in the steel which causes this passivity.

A Non-Magnetic Body

Stainless steels are further divided into four classes: martensitic, ferritic, austenitic and semi-austenitic. The alloy used in the De Lorean body is 304 and is austenitic, one result of which is that the body is non-magnetic. Austenitic chromium-nickel steels are also very tough through a wide range of temperatures.

You might by now be wondering, why isn't stainless steel used for other cars if it's such a good material? Simple, Although the ratio varies, the cost of stainless steel is usually five times that of the usual sheet metal steel.

The corrosion resistance of the DMC is called into question at times by owners, some of whom complain

DE LOREAN—matchless detail for comfort and convenience

It's called a cockpit, and for a very good reason. Every inch of the De Lorean's interior space has been carefully planned to provide optimum comfort and convenience: fully adjustable seats and power windows; a tilting, telescoping steering column; double weather seals, air conditioning and a seven position dual system of total climate control; full instrumentation and dual electric remote side view mirrors; variable speed windshield wiper/washer; extra storage space right behind the seats; centralized door locking and an AM/FM stereo cassette radio with a Dolby noise reduction system, electronic channel selection memory and digital frequency display. Truly an impressive array of standard features and equipment.

The interior is shown on this spread from the sales brochure. At the time it was produced (late 1980, for the '81 model year) the gray interior was not yet an option.

DE LOREAN—engineered for total performance

It's more than just the end result of clever engineering and good workmanship—total performance is the absolute standard against which each individual De Lorean component must be judged. A good example of this is the special treatment of the all-steel backbone chassis. It is actually sealed in fusion-bonded epoxy to protect it from corrosion. Or the way the 35/65 rear weight bias enables fully independent suspension to combine with rack and pinion steering for fast, sensitive handling response that needs no power assistance. To really let you feel the road—not just follow it!

Nestled within the rear arms of the rugged backbone chassis, there's a healthy and fuel-efficient 2.85 liter V6 power plant that employs Bosch K-Jetronic mechanical fuel injection and develops 130 SAE net horsepower at 5500 rpm. So whether you've selected the standard full synchro 5 speed transmission or the optional 3 speed automatic, you're in for a thoroughly rewarding experience when you drive a De Lorean.

Performance also means a 4-wheel disc braking system for progressive, fade-free stopping power. NCT steel belted radials for sure traction when it counts. Both of which become an integral part of the De Lorean driving experience.

DE LOREAN—anatomy of excellence

1981 De Lorean vehicle specifications

ENGINE
Type: light-alloy 90° V6 with overhead camshafts
Displacement: 2.85 liters (174 cu. in.)
Bore and stroke: 91 x 73mm
Compression ratio: 8.8:1
Block: light-alloy with cast iron cylinder liners
Heads: light-alloy, cross-flow hemi-chambers
Cooling system: water/ethylene glycol, forward radiator with two thermostatically controlled electric cooling fans
Fuel System: C.I.S. Bosch K-Jetronic mechanical fuel injection
Ignition system: breakerless, electronic Bosch
Emission control: Lambda-Sond catalytic, unleaded fuel

DRIVE TRAIN
Engine location: rear mounted
Transmission: 5 speed fully synchronized or 3 speed automatic
Final drive: transaxle/double universal half shafts, ratio 3.44:1

BODY AND CHASSIS
Underbody: composite structure
Outer panels: brushed stainless steel, grade 304
Construction: corrosion protected steel backbone frame, supporting cross members and 6-wheel independent suspension

SUSPENSION
Front: unequal length upper and lower control arms, coil springs, telescopic shocks and stabilizer bar
Rear: diagonal trailing radius arms with upper and lower links, coil springs with telescopic shocks

STEERING
Type: rack and pinion
Minimum turning radius: 5.18 meters (17.5')
Turning circle: 10.6M, curb-to-curb (35')
Wheel turns, lock to lock: 2.65

BRAKES
Type: power assisted discs, front and rear
Disc diameter: 251mm (10") front; 262mm (10.5") rear

Parking brake: mechanical, self-adjusting, acting on rear discs

WHEELS/TIRES
Wheels: cast light-alloy, 152mm x 152mm (14" x 6") front; 381mm x 203mm (15" x 8") rear
Tires: steel belted radial, Goodyear NCT

DIMENSIONS AND CAPACITIES
Wheelbase: 2409mm (94.8")
Track: 1590mm (62.6") front; 1588mm (62.5") rear
Length overall: 4221mm (168.0")
Width overall: 1988mm (78.3")
Height: 1140mm (44.88")
Weight, with full tank: 1218kg (2711 lbs.)
Fuel capacity: 51.8 liters (13.2 gal.)
Luggage capacity: 399 liters (16 cu. ft.)

ADDITIONAL STANDARD FEATURES
Stainless steel body panels
Counterbalanced gull-wing doors
Body side moldings
Tinted windows

Intermittent windshield wipers
Halogen headlamps
Engine/luggage compartment lights
Interior hood and engine compartment release

ADDITIONAL STANDARD EQUIPMENT
Air conditioning
AM-FM stereo radio w/cassette
Power windows
Central door locking system
Tilt and telescopic steering column
Dual electric remote side view mirrors
Cast light-alloy wheels
Electric rear window defogger
Electric tachometer
Locking gas cap

De Lorean Motor Company
2091 Sunburst Isles St.
Irvine, California 92714

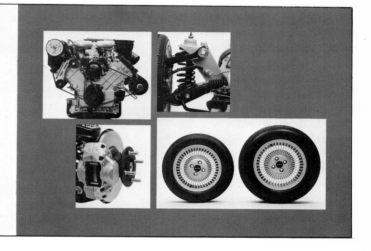

DE LOREAN—where it all comes together

The De Lorean Motor Company's assembly subsidiary is situated on a carefully planned 72 acre site in Dunmurry, Northern Ireland. Five major structures comprising more than 650,000 square feet have been designed and equipped exclusively for the assembly and testing of the De Lorean. But extensive use of advanced production technology is not the plant's only distinction.

Worker environment has been a special consideration at the De Lorean plant, from initial design through to production today. Unlike the traditional assembly method in which each worker repeats a single, monotonous task again and again, De Lorean employees perform several different jobs as members of a team. The absence of congestion and assembly-line pits add to pleasant working atmosphere. This extra attention to the personal satisfaction and pride of accomplishment of the De Lorean labor force is clearly reflected in a most tangible way: the consistently superior quality of workmanship you can expect to find in every De Lorean.

Total comfort, total performance, total commitment... totally De Lorean.

The brochure's technical content was not exhaustive, although the "backbone" chassis is shown to excellent advantage. Mention was not made of the engine's manufacturer.

Though there were several ads produced by other companies featuring either the car or the man (see pg. 108), only two DMC-sponsored ads appeared. This "Live the dream" 2-page color spread was produced by the Averett, Free & Fischer agency, and photographed by the renowned Art Kane. The ad ran in January, 1982 in publications such as Time, U.S. News & World Report *and the car enthusiast magazines. There was a strong difference of opinion within DMC about the type of advertising which should be used. John De Lorean preferred selling the image rather than product facts, hence this ad.*

that their De Lorean has rust spots! This would seem impossible, but can happen when an owner uses a ferrous metal pad to brush the stainless, leaving tiny particles of the ferrous metal in the surface, which will then rust. Scotchbrite pads from 3M are the suggested solution to this problem. The question of fingerprints also became another hassle, with a special treatment developed to eliminate it.

There are some problems with stainless steel. The most notable on the De Lorean are the aforementioned fingerprints, which sounds like a minor thing, but can detract a great deal from the car's appearance. There was a treatment developed to take care of the fingerprints, and as with any car a De Lorean has to be

washed regularly. For this the owner could buy a De Lorean Stainless Steel Car Care Kit, which included Stainless Steel Car Shampoo, Stainless Steel Cleaner/Sealer and Rubber, Leather, Vinyl Protector. Because the stainless also needs an occasional rebuffing the kit also had a De Lorean Stainless Steel Blending Pad.

The plastic caps that make up the area around the headlamps and taillights are a slightly darker shade than the stainless steel. It would be impossible to properly match the stainless and the color of the plastic, so it was decided that a slight contrast between the end caps and the metal was better than what appeared to be a color mismatch.

These are the factory's estimates of the time needed to remove and replace various panels and other items, such as mirrors or windshield. Trained De Lorean personnel are obviously assumed to be doing the work. (DMC)

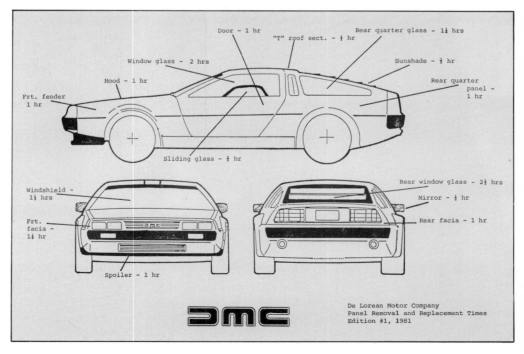

De Lorean Motor Company
Panel Removal and Replacement Times
Edition #1, 1981

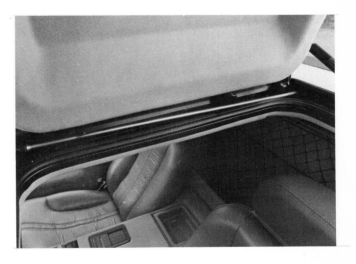

These photos show the complexity of the gullwing door seal, which leaked on early production models; as well as the "crysotwist" torsion bar which operates the counter-balanced gullwings. Setting of torsion bar tension may shift with temperature changes and require re-adjustment. Shock absorber strut (visible in upper right corner of both photos) slows rate at which door opens, prevents shocks to hinge mechanism. (Lamm)

Dubious feelings about the color of the *whole* car led some dealers to paint De Loreans, with mixed results, as it's difficult to make paint properly adhere to the stainless because of the oxide film we have mentioned. The factory preferred to attempt to retain some of the attraction of the stainless steel by adding color to it. They initiated a program with DuPont to develop a transparent coating over the stainless that would add color, but allow the brushed surface of the stainless to show through. Three cars were painted to test the process, and they looked very exciting, but it was found that under very humid conditions the paint would lift off the stainless surface. An undercoat would solve the lifting problem, but cover the look of the stainless steel.

A far more intriguing way John De Lorean considered for adding color to his sports car was with new body panels. Not stainless steel or metal, but soft urethane plastic bolted on in place of the metal panels. The plastic would not only add color but would be highly resistant to small dings and bumps to the body surface. We may not have heard the last of this bright idea.

The great unanswered question about the use of the stainless panels will take a few years to answer properly—how do you repair it? Unlike ordinary metal or fiberglass automobile bodies, any small dents, bumps or creases in the stainless sheetmetal cannot be simply pounded out, filled with lead or plastic filler, smoothed and then painted. Up to a point it is possible to remove a panel, bang out small dings and then rework the "brush marks" in the stainless. Entire body panels can (with considerable difficulty) be replaced, which is the obvious answer in major collisions . . . but the apparent failure of the De Lorean Motor Company may bring an end to the supply of stainless steel body panels. Now what?

The fiberglass underbody shouldn't be a serious problem to repair if damage isn't too severe, for while it is stressed, it needn't be finished for painting. Initially repair may be rather expensive, but in areas where De Lorean sales were high, De Lorean body repair specialists will probably establish themselves in the same manner fiberglass experts appeared to repair Corvettes.

Some Kind Of Arm Rest

Next on the list of the De Lorean's natural attractions are the gullwing doors. The early cars had a few fit problems stemming from the doors manufactured from pre-production "soft" dies. The striker plate guiding the door so it would latch had to be redesigned, because the first version required a downward pull precisely in the door's middle or it wouldn't close properly. De Loreans used in very cold climates sometimes have a problem when the gas struts meant to hold the door open don't really do the job. Another original hassle was the water seal of the doors, though a number of weatherstripping changes have

Instrument panel is conventional but complete, with full complement of warning lights and reminders. At front of center console is radio, heating/cooling vents and their controls, plus a well-placed digital clock. (Lamm)

solved most of this. For many owners those problems were tolerable to a point because of the advantages of the door's normal function, which is to allow driver and passenger to get in and out of the car in tight parking places, *and* draw the attention of people from across the parking lot or restaurant entrance to watch the driver (and passenger) arrive or leave in the De Lorean. Contained in each door's arm rest are a pull strap (or recess) to help slam the door, the door latch, the electric door lock, a switch on the driver's door for the electrically adjustable outside mirror and a vent to get some air conditioning air to the side of the interior. Some arm rest.

There remains, of course, the question of what happens to the doors in case of an accident. DMC claimed that during crash testing the instance of both doors jamming shut never occurred. What happens in an accident in which the car ends up upside down? DMC stated the chance of such an accident happening is slim, which is true, though it is a natural thought once you are closed up inside the gullwing door. The company said that when a car was placed upside down on its roof on a blacktop highway a 160-pound man was able to release the door and wiggle out. If both doors were jammed shut, DMC claimed it was possible to kick out the non-laminated safety glass side windows to escape.

Softer Interior Look

In contrast to the basically squared-off edges of the De Lorean's exterior, its interior is more soft and rounded and has a distinct Porsche 928 aura. In front of the driver is a 3-spoke steering wheel and ahead of that is the instrumentation: an 85-mph speedometer and 8,000-rpm tachometer are at the center of the panel, with smaller gauges for fuel level and oil pressure to their right and voltmeter and coolant temperature dials to their left. Warning lights on the instrument

A net-covered catch-all behind the seats serves as a good place for bags, small parcels, jackets etc. Gray interior colors help visually expand the size of the cockpit. (Lamm)

panel caution the driver about low oil pressure, insufficient volts from the alternator, a door that is ajar, a faulty brake system or handbrake, a problem with the oxygen sensor in the emissions system, low fuel level, if the headlights are on high- or low-beam; and give the usual seatbelt, hazard and directional reminders.

Porsche 928

This is a Porsche 928 interior, and the De Lorean has the same soft, rounded, cushioned look and feel to it, which is quite a compliment in the sense that the Porsche is a $43,000 super car. It's a shame the De Lorean didn't live long enough to benefit from the same kind of development the Porsche has received.

Seats are covered in Bridge of Weir leather; door panels and dashboard in a soft, pliable vinyl. (Lamm)

On early production cars the hood had to be raised to access the gas filler, making spillage on luggage or packages a real possibility, so one of the first running changes was the addition of a gas filler cap. (Lamm)

Luggage area up front holds four cubic feet by R&T *measurement, and is shallow as well. Motor-driven radio antenna sprouts from between louvers of air intake at rear of car.* (Lamm)

Stalks on the steering column contain the switches for light and windshield wiper/washer functions.

Mounted on the tall center console between driver and passenger is the shift lever, cigarette lighter, an ashtray and a row of buttons to control the windows and the rear window defroster. At the front of the console is the stereo radio/tape deck, placed between the center vents for the heating/cooling system and the controls for that system.

At the right of the dashboard is a glovebox, while behind the seats is an area for small bags, jackets and such, to be held in place by an elastic netting. The dashboard and door panels are covered with a very soft, pliable vinyl. The seats are upholstered in a similar sort of loose tuck fit with leather from Scotland's Isle of Weir, and the look is soft and round in the manner of a space-age easy chair. Early De Loreans had their interiors finished in black, which did a great deal to heighten the claustrophobic feeling inside the car, a sensation that was lessened in later cars with their gray interiors. Mounted on the floor to the driver's left is the emergency brake handle.

Ahead of the passenger compartment is the luggage area which has, by the measurements of *Road & Track* magazine, only 4 cubic feet. It's also rather shallow, making narrow soft luggage advisable. Under the front lid on the earlier cars is the fuel filler, so the nozzle must be handled carefully to keep gasoline off the luggage. After the first several hundred cars, a separate small door in the left-rear of the hood was added to the fuel filler.

Backbone Chassis And Suspension

The stainless steel panels are, of course, attached to the fiberglass underbody, which is in turn mounted at 10 points to the backbone chassis. The heart of the 95.0-inch wheelbase chassis is its backbone welded up of mild steel, with the center section leading to a "Y"

"Backbone" chassis is welded from mild steel and epoxy coated for rustproofing. The design is simple, strong and very effective functionally. Radiator mounting structure has crush tubes which slow deformation in an accident, and gas tank is well-protected. (Lamm)

shape both front and rear. At the front, the "Y" ends are joined by a structure that continues forward to locate the radiator and the crush tubes which slow the vehicle's deformation in case of an accident. Wing-like towers sprout out to the sides to hold the top of the shock absorbers. The rear "Y" also ends at shock towers, which then continue down and under in a wide U-shape crossmember forming the bottom of the engine bay. The rear periphery of the bay is formed by a 3-sided rectangle. This backbone structure is heated and dipped in a liquidized epoxy powder which slips into all the nooks and crannies, completely coating the frame and providing what De Lorean unofficially claims is 25 years of protection.

Fitted in the forward "Y" is the plastic gas tank, such location keeping it about as well protected in an accident as possible. Mounted out front are the radiator and a like-size air conditioning condenser. The radiator plumbing is routed back into the "Y," where it runs encased back to the engine. Just ahead of the crossbrace that connects the front points of the "Y" is the rack and pinion steering. The front suspension has an A-arm at the top connecting the shock tower and the wheel spindle. At the bottom a single arm runs

Upper A-arm connects shock tower to wheel spindle, single arm does same below. Anti-roll bar connects to lower arm. (Lamm)

from tower to spindle. That takes care of up-down movement, while fore-aft control is meant to be handled by the anti-roll bar, which runs forward and is connected to the frame just behind the radiator.

Like the front suspension, the rear suspension

(LEFT) The compact V-6 engine transmission is built by a Peugeot-Renault-Volvo consortium. (DMC) (OPPOSITE): The data panel from the Road & Track *road test appearing in the December 1981 issue. (Courtesy* Road & Track *magazine)*

follows basic Lotus practice. The wheel hub is attached through two lateral arms to provide the correct vertical movement, while a long semi-trailing arm—which is attached well forward at the base of the rear "Y"—holds the hub in correct fore-aft position. Both the front 10.0-inch and the rear 10.5-inch power-assisted disc brakes are mounted at the wheel. On the forward wheels are 195/60HR-14 Goodyear NCT tires, while the rears are large 235/60HR-15 tires, both mounted on aluminum alloy wheels.

PRV Engine And Renault Gearbox

Nestled in the rear "Y," facing to the rear, is the Peugeot-Renault-Volvo single-overhead camshaft V-6. In its De Lorean form, the aluminum V-6 has 130 bhp at 5500 rpm and 160 lb-ft of torque at 2750 rpm, just

as it does in Volvo sedans. Mounted ahead of the engine is the transmission, either a 5-speed manual or 3-speed automatic. Both gearboxes are used in the Renault Fuego, which is sold in the U.S., making replacement transmission parts as readily available as those for the engine.

Initially the choice of transmission was the only choice a De Lorean buyer had to make, because the automatic transmission was the only option. Late in 1981 another option was offered, that being a gray interior instead of the black. The lighter shade does reduce the world-is-closing-in-on-me feeling of the coal mine interior. Burgundy and saddle brown interior colors were to be future options. There was also a short list of dealer-added options offered by DMC, including a ski rack, side stripes, a luggage rack, floor mats, a

A good view of the engine installation and simple rear suspension arrangement. This happens to be the experimental stainless steel chassis which was fabricated to test the feasibility of doing so in future. Expensive. (DMC)

R&T ROAD TEST
DELOREAN

SCALE: 10 in. (254 mm) DIVISIONS

PRICE

List price, all POE $25,000
Price as tested $25,000
    Price as tested includes std equip (air cond, AM/
FM stereo/cassette, leather seats, elect. lifts for
partial windows, elect. mirrors, stainless steel body
finish)

MANUFACTURER

DeLorean Motor Co, 280 Park Avenue, 43rd Floor,
New York, N.Y. 10017

GENERAL

Curb weight, lb/kg ....2840................1288
Test weight ....3130................1420
Weight dist (with driver), f/r, % 38/62
Wheelbase, in./mm ....94.8................2408
Track, front/rear ....62.6/62.5....1590/1588
Length ....168.0................4267
Width ....78.3................1990
Height ....44.9................1140
Ground clearance ....5.6..................142
Overhang, f/r ....35.3/37.9.......897/962
Trunk space, cu ft/liters ....4.0..................113
Fuel capacity, U.S. gal./liters ....13.5................51

ACCOMMODATION

Seating capacity, persons 2
Head room, in./mm ....34.0................864
Seat width ....2 x 18.5.......2 x 470
Seatback adjustment, deg 45

ENGINE

Type ....sohc V-6
Bore x stroke, in./mm ...3.58 x 2.87 ...91.0 x 73.0
Displacement, cu in./cc ....174............2849
Compression ratio 8.8:1
Bhp @ rpm, SAE net/kW ....130/97 @ 5500
   Equivalent mph / km/h 136/219
Torque @ rpm, lb-ft/Nm ......162/220 @ 2750
   Equivalent mph / km/h 69/111
Fuel injection ....Bosch K-Jetronic
Fuel requirement........................unleaded, 91-oct
Exhaust-emission control equipment: 3-way catalyst,
oxygen sensor

DRIVETRAIN

Transmission ....5-sp manual
Gear ratios: 5th (0.82) 2.82:1
   4th (1.06) 3.65:1
   3rd (1.38)...4.75:1
   2nd (2.06) 7.10:1
   1st (3.36) 11.56:1
Final drive ratio 3.44:1

INSTRUMENTATION

Instruments: 85-mph speedo, 8000-rpm tach,
  99,999.9 odo, 999.9 trip odo, oil press., coolant
  temp, voltmeter, fuel level, clock
Warning lights: oil press., brake sys/handbrake, alternator, oxygen sensor, low fuel, door ajar, rear-
  window heat, seatbelts, hazard, high beam, low
  beam, directionals

CHASSIS & BODY

Layout ....rear engine/rear drive
Body/frame ....steel backbone frame,
  separate fiberglass and stainless steel body
Brake system ....10.0-in. (254-mm) discs front,
  10.5-in. (267-mm) discs rear; vacuum assisted
Swept area, sq in./sq cm ....541................3490
Wheels ....cast alloy, 14 x 6 front, 15 x 8 rear
Tires....Goodyear NCT; 195/60HR-14 front, 235/60HR-
  15 rear
Steering type ....rack & pinion
  Overall ratio ....na
  Turns, lock-to-lock 3.2
  Turning circle, ft/m ....30.0 ....9.1
Front suspension: unequal-length A-arms, coil springs,
  tube shocks, anti-roll bar
Rear suspension: semi-trailing arms, upper and lower
  lateral arms, coil springs, tube shocks

MAINTENANCE

Service intervals, mi:
  Oil/filter change 7500/7500
  Chassis lube ....none
  Tuneup.......................................30,000
Warranty, mo/mi 12/12,000

CALCULATED DATA

Lb/bhp (test weight) 24.1
Mph/1000 rpm (5th gear)............................25.0
Engine revs/mi (60 mph) 2400
Piston travel, ft/mi...................................1195
R&T steering index...................................0.96
Brake swept area, sq in./ton 346

ROAD TEST RESULTS

ACCELERATION

Time to distance, sec:
  0-100 ft 3.4
  0-500 ft 9.5
  0-1320 ft (¼ mi) 17.9
Speed at end of ¼ mi, mph 76.5
Time to speed, sec:
  0-30 mph 3.6
  0-60 mph 10.5
  0-100 mph 40.0

SPEEDS IN GEARS

5th gear (4400 rpm) 109
4th (5600) 109
3rd (6500)..98
2nd (6500) 64
1st (6500) 40

FUEL ECONOMY

Normal driving, mpg 19.5
Cruising range, mi (1-gal. res) 244

HANDLING

Lateral accel, 100-ft radius, g 0.772
Speed thru 700-ft slalom, mph 59.7

BRAKES

Minimum stopping distances, ft:
  From 60 mph 158
  From 80 mph 260
Control in panic stop ....fair
Pedal effort for 0.5g stop, lb 25
Fade: percent increase in pedal effort
  to maintain 0.5g deceleration in 6
  stops from 60 mph....................nil
Parking: hold 30% grade? ....yes
Overall brake rating.............very good

INTERIOR NOISE

Idle in neutral, dBA 63
Maximum, 1st gear 82
Constant 30 mph 70
  50 mph 75
  70 mph 78

SPEEDOMETER ERROR

30 mph indicated is actually........30.0
60 mph 57.0
80 mph 75.0

ACCELERATION

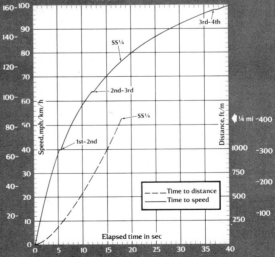

Image was critical to the entire De Lorean project, and a number of companies felt John De Lorean and his company were right for their image too. The net result was a bonanza of free media exposure of a very high caliber and a great boost for a fledgling company's credibility.

car cover and sheepskin seat covers. In the works before DMC fell on hard times were projects for De Lorean sunglasses, watches, perfume . . . the list could have been endless.

Early Problems

Like all new cars the De Lorean wasn't totally without fault as introduced. There were a total of four recalls on the car by the factory. One involved the throttle sticking open in cold weather when water could enter and freeze in what is called a throttle spool. A plate designed to deflect water away from the spool solved that problem. Two recalls involved the front suspension; the initial recall—which covered about 350 cars—occurred after two cars suffered a collapsed suspension when a nut holding part of the front wheel broke. In the third recall, other nuts in the front suspension were suspected of backing off and had to be replaced with castellated nuts, which have a hole through them that allows them to be pinned in place. There was even a minor recall of the castle nuts before everything was finished, but the recall, which involved around 2,200 cars was finally completed. The fourth recall came in late Spring, 1982, for a device called an inertia switch. Every modern car sold in the U.S. with an electric fuel pump has such a switch which is designed to shut off the fuel pump in the case of a roll-over accident to minimize the chance of fire. The switch supplier delivered a batch of defective ones to DMC that would cut-out without warning, so the inertia switches were replaced in all De Loreans.

There were other questions about the front suspension in addition to the recalls. Following Esprit practice, the suspension has a single lower control arm connecting the frame to the wheel. Fore-aft movement of the control arm is limited by a device called the anti-roll bar. This bar connects one front wheel to the other and prevents, as its name implies, body roll by the car

Sylvania promoted its line of halogen headlights with this ad in Road & Track.

Undoubtedly the best known De Lorean ad, repeatedly used in leading consumer magazines. The copy recalls De Lorean's GM success.

Attracting wide attention, the 1981 American Express Christmas catalog offered a De Lorean "electroplated with pure 24 karat gold" at $85,000—but you could charge it. Two of the planned 100 were sold, one in Texas, the other in California (where else?).

Goodyear NCT tires are used on De Loreans, and the headline on this full color double page ad probably makes the Goodyear marketing men cringe today.

Some De Lorean owners have lowered their cars (left) by cutting four inches from the back springs and then swapping back springs with front. It does improve the looks without any apparent penalty in handling or ride.
(R. A. McCormack)

during cornering. In the De Lorean, the bar is behind the radiator, and each end is curved back so the ends of the bar are attached at the lower control arm. The bar is attached to the chassis through rubber bushings to isolate noise and permit the suspension to move somewhat—otherwise the ride of the car would be rock hard. However, the suspension must only work in certain directions or such movement can allow the wheels to take angles that could adversely affect handling and stability. To some engineers at De Lorean, the Lotus design allowed the anti-roll bar and bushing to flex too much, allowing the front wheels to turn sufficiently outward under braking to cause some instability. Harder bushings would have been one means of minimizing the movement. There was even thought given to triangulate the lower arm to prevent the movement fore and aft, which is another simple fix.

Turbocharging From Legend Industries

Another change, one that was being looked into even as the De Lorean was starting production, was adding some power to the PRV V-6 engine. With the automotive magazine road tests showing 0-60 mph times between 9.5-10.5 seconds for the stainless steel sports car when all the car's serious rivals were in the 7.5-8.5 second range, the need is obvious. The owners may not go that fast themselves, but they do read the automotive magazines to compare acceleration figures and then it matters.

From the start of the engineering program for the De Lorean there had been interest in a turbocharged engine as a natural route for the company to follow in looking for more horsepower. There was already a De Lorean version of the V-6 with a pair of turbos on display with the car when it was shown at the National Automobile Dealers Association meeting in Los Angeles in January, 1980.

With Mike Loasby and the rest of the DMC

The twin-turbo engine developed for DMC by Legend Industries. R & T editor John Dinkel drove the car and calls it "fantastic," comparing acceleration to Porsche 930 Turbo. (DMC)

engineering staff already busy with other projects, De Lorean again decided to go outside for help in developing the turbo version of his car. Legend Industries of Hauppauge, New York, already had an excellent reputation for their turbocharging systems. They were the company retained to turn the aging Fiat spider 2000 into a pleasant 1980's sports car with one of their turbo installations. The car De Lorean asked Legend to develop was to have added horsepower, to be produced without a great sacrifice in fuel economy. DMC also wanted a turbo that provided a wide power band, and not the sort of peaky surge of power one gets in a Porsche 930 Turbo. Naturally, the turbo system couldn't do anything to cut into the De Lorean's durability, and it had to be easy to service.

The Bosch K-Jetronic fuel injection already on the V-6 was a natural for the turbo installation, so that wasn't changed. Legend then added a pair of I.H.I.

One of first independent De Lorean specialists is Sun Enterprises in Westminster, California, run by former QAC mgr. Joe Black (left) with ex-DMC employees (L to R) Don Eitleman, Al Agee, Rick Fuller, Ruong Nguyen, Nick Hurtado, Dave Ryckman, and Carol Richardson. Due to stress beyond design limits Black predicts problems with door lock solenoids, window motors, alternator, fuel pump and coolant overflow bottle. (Lamm)

(that stands for Ishikawajimi-Harima Heavy Industries, so you know why they just use their initials) RHB52 turbos. A pair of these was preferable to one large turbo because their small size made packaging easier and Legend was able to tuck them down low near the exhaust ports, keeping exhaust valve-to-turbine and compressor-to-intake-valve distances as short as possible. Small turbos also meant less rotating inertia, which helps reponse time. Between the turbochargers and the throttle body of the fuel injection is a pair of intercoolers. These cool the air headed for the engine and are helpful because a cooler, dense charge is more efficient and keeps combustion chamber temperatures down, which helps prevent destructive detonation in the chamber.

Naturally a number of owners weren't about to wait for the factory to do their turbo installation and several of them had turbochargers added to their De Loreans. Andy Weiss, head of the 200-member De Lorean Motor Car Club of Southern California, reports that another common modification is to replace the 1.5-inch exhaust piping with 2.0-inch pipe, which lowers back pressure, adds a bit of horsepower, ups fuel mileage somewhat, ". . . and makes the car sound a lot better."

Another modification curing a common complaint is one that lowers the De Lorean on its suspension. The coil springs normally at the front of the De Lorean are moved to the rear suspension, while those from the back are cut down by about 4.0 inches. The result improves both the car's appearance and purportedly its handling. Some owners have also made the switch from Goodyear tires to the Pirelli P7's around which the original prototype was designed. No question about the value of that change. And on occasion the change was made because a number of early De Loreans were delivered with the front suspension toe-in incorrectly set, causing very quick tire wear.

Some Common Problems

As a De Lorean club president, Weiss can also recite the major problems the car's owners suffer. The original clutch pedal design didn't allow for any adjustment, eventually making it difficult for the driver to cleanly shift from gear to gear. The fix involved adding a clevis to the end of the clutch cable to allow adjustment. Brake rotors warped on some cars, requiring replacement. There were a few problems with the electrically operated door locks which could cause the driver to be locked inside his De Lorean. To get at the wiring that causes this failure means taking off the roof sheetmetal, which is a problem in itself. Weiss claims he rarely locks his car when he's inside it. The instruments, particularly the speedometer and its cables, have been somewhat problematical. And the rain drain from the front window can route water over the electrical fuel pump, causing it to rust and pack up.

Most of the hassles suffered by De Lorean owners have been minor but frustrating, a situation made even more so by dealers who were reluctant (rightly so in some cases) to do warranty work on the De Loreans as long as DMC owed them money for past warranty claims. There is also the question of some dealerships not being able to do the work properly. Some of the blame for this must fall back on DMC, which produced a parts book and another volume on how the car works, but never a proper service manual. The lack of good service was particularly annoying for the owners who had bought early De Loreans . . . they paid the most money and also had the most problems.

With the failure of DMC comes the problem of where the owners will get any parts at all, much less have their cars serviced properly. Because the De Lorean is an assembly of parts many will be

As dealer stocks mounted, the $25,000 list price nose-dived. This ad appeared in Southern California in October, 1982. A year earlier some eager buyers had paid as much as $29,000. At first dealer cost was $19,000, but this was subsequently discounted in various ways. As exclusive distributor, DMC paid the factory (DMC Ltd.) about $16,500. Factory cost was about $13,500.

available, such as the engine/gearbox from Renault. When you get to the pieces that were made specifically for De Lorean things can get tighter. And what of the stainless steel body panels? Will they eventually have to be replaced with fiberglass copies and then painted?

Luckily for De Lorean owners, Consolidated will continue in the De Lorean parts business. Jeff Abrams, who headed Consolidated's contingent during its long, hard look at possibly saving the Northern Ireland factory, made certain component production was continued to stockpile many De Lorean parts. Just how long they will last is uncertain, but Abrams had an additional 1,000 pairs of doors produced, this being the most complex and difficult part to replace. He also continued production of body panels and will be able to carry on making hoods in the U.S. Consolidated will have a supply of wheels and tires, along with almost 500 engine/tranmission units that were bought from Renault. Still, some parts, such as center consoles, will be difficult to get in the future. As an interesting aside, Abrams owns the first and last De Loreans produced. (Alright trivia fans, if you must know the first was built on January 21, 1981 and is Chassis No. BD000500, with the last being built December 24, 1982 and Chassis No. DD0020104.)

Nobody ever said it's easy to own an exotic car. The ironic part is that one aim of project management—whether John De Lorean, Bill Collins, Mike Kimberley, or Mike Loasby—was to produce an exotic car that wouldn't be a hassle for owners. There would be a large dealer network and enough De Loreans on the road to make parts and service available throughout the country and, with luck, the world. However, if you should bend the sheetmetal on your De Lorean and want it to look like new, especially as the world's supply of stainless steel De Lorean body panels diminishes, you may find out that unbending a Ferrari or Rolls Royce is child's play by comparison.

COLOR SALON #2
The Production Car

The Lotus VARI process (Vacuum Assist Resin Injection) requires a wooden pattern from which a mold is cast.

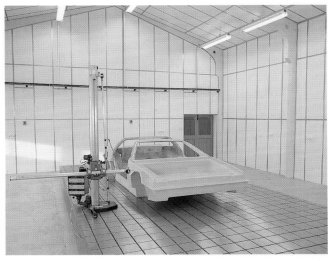

Measurements for the VARI pattern were taken from this full scale model, housed in one of the converted hangars.

Orange De Lorean at far left is one of 18 test vehicles with fiberglass bodies built by Lotus to permit immediate chassis development work rather than wait for steel panels. (Group Lotus) Brilliant Lotus founder Colin Chapman, shown above in 1978 with Mario Andretti and Ronnie Peterson, suffered a heart attack and died on December 16, 1982, at the age of 54. (Lamm)

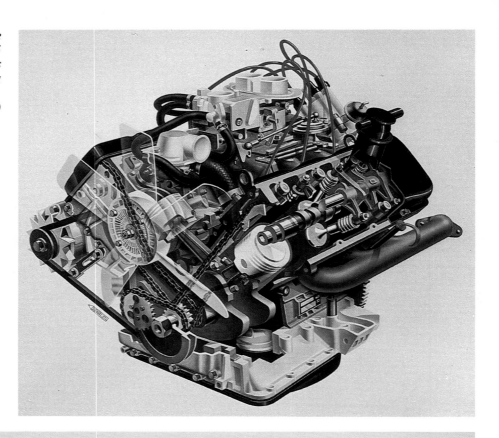

Renault/Volvo/Peugeot engine is alloy V-6 displacing 2.85 litres (174 cid) and produces 130 hp @ 5500 rpm using Bosch K-Jetronic fuel injection. (Renault)

Under The Skin

Forty-five major suppliers from eight countries provided the parts for the De Lorean, all well-known and from the top echelon, such as Harrison Radiator, GTE, Lucas Girling, Delco Remy, Saginaw Steering Gear, GKN, Bridge of Weir Leather Co., BSC Stainless, Rockwell International, AC Spark Plug, Robert Bosch, etc. Future parts availability should be good, especially in view of Consolidated International's efforts to build and stockpile components, particularly the unique stainless panels. This cutaway drawing appears in the owner's manual, which is thorough and well-done. There was no shop manual as such, but a book of parts drawings and companion piece with system descriptions was produced and can be obtained from the owners' clubs.

Lotus "backbone" chassis is an engineering masterstroke of Colin Chapman which he first used in the 1964 Elan, and for all subsequent Lotus road cars. However, De Lorean was the first true rear engine car to which Lotus applied the idea (Lotus Europa is mid-engine). Rear weight bias is 35/65, and 14" x 6" tires are used in front, 15" x 8" at rear. (Lamm)

Photo above shows a "pre-production" De Lorean, identifiable because of the simple sliding side window scheme, which in hindsight was probably a better idea than the production car's small, motorized "toll-booth" window. At least with the sliding window you can blast along and let the wind in to muss your hair if you wish. (DMC)
LEFT: Peter Moore of the DMC staff in Northern Ireland poses beside one of the preview cars made available for the press tour. (DMC)

Inspiration for all gullwings, the Mercedes-Benz 300 SL still remains in a class by itself by virtue of its racing heritage. (Lamm)

*Being a structural member,
De Lorean door is much thicker than
300 SL, and must contain window
motors, etc. (Lamm)*

Soft gray leather interior is perfect complement to the stainless steel exterior. The magic of the De Lorean is captured well in the photos below and opposite. During the last quarter of 1981 De Lorean outsold the Porsche 911SC (2499 to 1299), Porsche 924 (1062), Porsche Turbo 924 (602), and did almost as well as the Mercedes 380SL (2913). (Lamm)

De Loreans look wonderful in color, as these photos of privately painted cars demonstrate. Had the company continued, color as well as the stainless steel exterior would have been offered. (Photos above, John Lamm. At right, Jeff Pollack.)

8

Facing The Critics

TWO OF THE GREATEST dangers any automotive journalist can face are to become stale and cynical. Unlike some forms of journalism in which cynicism is almost a necessity, those who write about cars have to remain wary but open-minded. Develop a hardened, snide attitude about which automakers are perpetual losers and winners and it will come back to haunt you. The revival of Mazda and Subaru from their failures of the early Seventies are proof of the former, while the decline of Detroit at the end of that decade and into the early Eighties points up the latter. On the other hand, it would be crazy to call the U.S. automakers down and out.

At the beginning of 1981, however, the story of John Z. De Lorean and his automobile threatened to make many automotive writers both stale and cynical. It had little to do with Bricklins or any of the many promises we'd all heard from various automotive entrepreneurs over the years. And De Lorean's personal creditability wasn't suffering, it was just that after years of promises and missed production dates from many automakers large and small, one is reluctant to do or say anything about a new car until it's possible to touch, smell, see, hear, and drive it.

As of January 1, 1981, no writer had been able to do any sort of proper driving of a De Lorean. We could see, touch and smell prototype De Loreans, but even during the pre-release photography sessions—a common practice among automakers to accommodate the magazines' lead time—the photographers weren't allowed to drive the De Lorean they were shooting.

One More Postponement

To make us even more wary, the initial press trip to Ireland, during which writers would be travelling with John De Lorean, have an opportunity to see the factory, and also drive the car for the first time, was

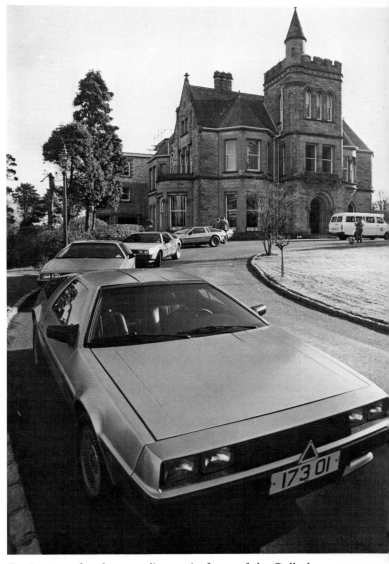

De Loreans for the press line up in front of the Culloden Hotel in the Holywood suburb of Belfast. (DMC)

postponed from the middle of February, 1981, until March . . . another postponement, another magazine issue gone before the De Lorean could be driven, another promise put off. The reasons from the De Lorean Motor Company were logical enough, because they wanted to make certain the cars were completely ready for their debut, and various production start-up delays had caused problems with the early cars. Few writers would argue much with that, because none of them wanted an unrepresentative automobile for driving impressions, but the postponement did little to squelch an increasingly cynical tone among De Lorean's critics.

However, come March a group of six journalists gathered in New York's Kennedy International Airport for the first official press junket to see, smell, touch and drive the De Lorean Sports Car. On the TWA flight with De Lorean were seven journalists from the U.S.: Tom Bryant from *Road & Track;* Don Sherman of *Car and Driver;* John Dianna, representing both *Motor Trend* and *Sports Car Graphic;* Gary Witzenberg, a freelance writer working this time for *Playboy;* George Levy from *Autoweek;* Tony Ascenza of *Popular Mechanics;* and *Popular Science*'s Ed Jacobs. Tony Swann, also from *Motor Trend* and *Sports Car Graphic* met the group in London.

From the start of his project, De Lorean had said how important he considered the impressions of the major automotive magazines, and their influence in forming public opinion about any new automobile. Porsche, Mercedes-Benz, BMW and other companies that sell expensive automobiles share this same view, hence the press junket.

At London's Heathrow International Airport the journalists had their first indication they weren't headed for a normal European city. As is standard procedure on British Airways' Belfast Shuttle, their carry-on hand luggage was carefully searched. Unlike most searches, however, this one did not include returning the camera bags and such, but instead they were put into plastic bags, sealed and then sent off to the baggage hold. This careful security treatment is just another carry-over from the Battle of the Boyne in 1690 and the start of the "Troubles," and for anyone travelling to Belfast it is the first of many little reminders of the Northern Ireland problem. In total they underscore how unusual it is for a new manfacturing company to begin life in Belfast, unlike the many established companies—the Ford Motor Company being one example—with a plant in Northern Ireland. The "Troubles" also account for the generous incentives offered to industries that will settle in Northern Ireland.

Flying into Belfast (as I did on a later visit), it isn't difficult to see the beauty of Northern Ireland. Even in March when the group arrived there was more than enough green to back up all the comments about Ireland being the Emerald Isle. Once past the British checkpoint outside the airport—a station meant to check for, among other things, devices hanging down under the car—the feeling is of rural England. The route to the De Lorean factory includes a stretch of the infamous Dundrod race course, no longer used, but once one of the most dangerous road circuits in Europe. For the next three days the group had a chance to see Ireland, tour the De Lorean factory and, at long last, drive the De Lorean.

Put Up Or Shut Up

It was put up or shut up time. As Don Sherman described his thoughts before this first drive, "John Z. has always been one of those swashbuckling, shoot-from-the-hip types, destined for stardom if not success. His car—up to now—has also been ethereal. It was on the verge of becoming the perpetual prototype—once an ethical, safety sports car, then a

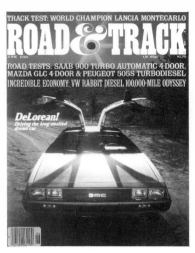

nouveau Lotus—always resisting the freeze into something solid.''

The factory didn't get much comment from the writers in their subsequent articles, despite the amazingly short time spent taking it from an empty green field to a fully operational plant. Fair enough, considering they were writing for automotive journals, not engineering magazines. Tom Bryant did a short section in his story describing the factory tour, noting that it ''looks more like an electronics plant than a car factory. . . .''

After the usual amenities, including a short familiarization drive on the factory's compact test track, the writers began their 1 1/2-day test drive around Northern Ireland, ''. . . challenging the narrow roads, Irish drivers and free-spirited sheep,'' as Bryant later described it. There were four cars for the eight journalists, two each with the 3-speed automatic and 5-speed manual transmissions.

In the end, reviews from the big three automotive magazines were mixed. Swann seemed the most impressed. Writing in the June, 1981, *Motor Trend,* he summed up the styling by saying, ''Although the look is on the verge of becoming just a bit dated, it remains slippery . . . and distinctive.'' After a comment on the minimal visibility to the rear from inside the car (a common problem in rear- and mid-engine cars), he went on to give the interior good marks: ''Inside, the trim is spare but of high quality, reminiscent in some ways of the Porsche approach [high praise in the De Lorean's market segment—Ed.]. The seats are well shaped and snug, and the instruments are small but neatly arranged in the fascia cowling with a good sight line through the steering wheel.''

How Fast Is Fast?

Acceleration is always a difficult area for a writer to comment on. One hates to say too much without knowing the 0–60 mph time as determined by the magazine's road tester and all his magic equipment. Then again, after a point the seconds aren't *that* important if the subjective feel of the car fits its image. Swann commented on the De Lorean by saying that ''there's plenty of power to go with the sleek exterior. Even in full U.S. exhaust emission trim, the Renault V-6 with Volvo cylinder heads and Bosch fuel injection packs plenty of torque.'' He also liked the steering, brakes and gearbox. (''The 5-speed . . . has short throws, and the ratios are well-spaced with low-rpm cruising available in 5th gear.'') As for the handling, Swann noted that the driver is aware of the mass hung out back (''. . . the Porsche-like impression of engine noise trying—but never quite succeeding—to catch up''), but he didn't feel it adversely affected the De Lorean's handling in the way most writers suspected: oversteer, when the back of the car is overly sensitive to sliding out when the car is driven close to its handling limits.

Tom Bryant, writing in *Road & Track* (June, 1981), began his driving impressions section by saying that when he first saw the car in Dunmurry he thought, ''What a handsome car.'' He added, ''. . . there's no denying the De Lorean is an excitingly sleek sports car that reflects the Giugiaro look of flat surfaces and sharp edges prevalent at the time it was designed.'' He commented most about the doors: ''The gullwing doors may be considered impractical by some . . . but there's no denying they add visual excitement and exclusivity.'' He seemed to generally like the De Lorean's interior, and being a tall man himself, Bryant appreciated the amount of interior room and seat adjustability of the car. After also commenting on the limited outward vision, he added another wrinkle to the De Lorean's interior, saying, ''Another sensation that results from the interior design is a slight sense of claustrophobia. Sitting low, surrounded by lots of black upholstery, and with limited outward vision, I found myself feeling a bit hemmed in. . . ."

Although Bryant obviously enjoyed a chance to take a shot at the De Lorean's claimed top speed of around 130 mph, he wasn't as impressed with the car's acceleration. "With 130 bhp and 162 lb-ft torque, the De Lorean is not a tire-burner off the line, and while I would characterize it as a fairly fast car, it's not an especially quick one. Again, the factory claims a 0–60 mph time between 9–10 seconds and I would say that's likely."

As for driving, Bryant said, "The handling characteristics are somewhat disappointing, as the De Lorean is not a car you immediately feel at home in, but rather one that takes some getting used to." After describing the ride as being ". . . appropriately firm without being jiggly . . ." he was surprised to find ". . . an initial dose of body roll, combining with light steering effort, to lead to imprecision in finding the best line through the corner. Understeer is the dominant characteristic, ranging from near neutral at low speeds to mild as the car approaches its limits, never crossing into oversteer, which would be quite a handful with the rear weight bias. Once accustomed to the car, however, I found I was able to hustle it along at a good clip, never getting the rear end to break adhesion. . . ."

Flat On His Face

Road & Track's article concluded, "I wanted to like the De Lorean Sports Car very much, simply because it looks right, uses a variety of new and exciting materials and production techniques, and because a successful new carmaker could bring needed fresh thinking to the U.S. market." After adding that he didn't think the car's $25,000 price tag would be a problem, Bryant finished, "It's going to be a long,

arduous process, and there are many people, particularly in Detroit, who are hoping John De Lorean will fall flat on his face. On the other hand, lots of people in Northern Ireland, and lots of taxpayers in Great Britain, who put up millions of pounds in loans and grants, are rooting for a De Lorean victory. Only time will tell."

Don Sherman wrote about the De Lorean in *Car and Driver*'s May, 1981, issue, offering an overview and a number of photographs, but no driving impressions. *C/D* had tired of waiting for the trip to Ireland to materialize and decided to use a basic story first. They followed it up in July with Sherman's full story about the junket to Belfast.

As the magazine's Technical Director, Sherman began his story by relating the luxury of the trip, then saying, "A cortege of distinguished American motor-journalists has been diddled again; every one of us is rushing back to the typewriter with more questions than answers." After commenting on the fact that DMC was beginning life building what he figured was one of the most complex automobiles in the world, Sherman summarized his feelings about the car early in the story by saying, "It's a pity the De Lorean is so tough to build at the moment, because our first impressions are overwhelmingly positive. Giugiaro's rounded-doorstop sculpture looks magnificent in the flesh, and the machinery is good enough to spark a fiery love affair after one quick drive around the block. The De Lorean is not a hard-edged answer to the 911 Porsche, nor is it another fatuous Corvette-clone. And while it stretches the established sports-car performance envelope not an iota, this car is at least happy with itself. The handling is safe and satisfying, the V-6 engine surprisingly mellow in its newest assignment. The interior is roomy, comfortable, and reasonably well thought out. Most important, the De Lorean passes the critical enthusiast's test: it's fun to drive."

After commenting on the "entombed" feeling of the interior and adding that it's ". . . darker than a snake pit inside . . ." Sherman went on to comment favorably about the layout of the instruments and various controls and switches, only really questioning some aspects of the seating. He said of the engine, "The 130-horsepower, fuel-injected V-6 packed away back in the De Lorean's tail is probably the best-behaved part of the car." The gearing in both the 5-speed manual and 3-speed automatic transmission cars was too tall for his tastes and left the midrange acceleration "sluggish." He added that it didn't help that ". . . at an advertised 2,700 pounds, the De Lorean is 10 percent overweight for the lean life of the Eighties."

Pitch-It-And-Punch-It

Even the handling of the De Lorean was to Sherman's liking: "Long ago, when all the doomsayers noticed that a good share of the De Lorean's mass is positioned high and just inboard of the back bumper, they gazed nervously into the future and foresaw treacherous oversteer. Alas, their concerns are unfounded. There's been so much engineering attention to rear-engine shortcomings that most have become attributes." Those qualities are light steering, impressive stopping and added luggage spaces. "Oversteer, either on or off the power, is factored out with a drastic differential between front and rear tire sizes, inflation pressures and wheel widths. Furthermore, roll stiffness is biased in such a way that front traction always fades first. Our early pitch-it-and-punch-it stunts on local roundabouts (both wet and dry) could never dissuade the De Lorean from a nose-first plunge to (and through) the limit." Quite a compliment for Colin Spooner of Lotus, who deserves credit for much of the development work on the De Lorean.

Now all this was *very* positive stuff, but it was tempered at its end by questions about the quality of the car, stemming from the difficulty in building the gullwing doors. Sherman suggested the first 500 cars (those made with the Kirksite dies) should become permanent, doors-open displays at De Lorean dealers. He ended saying: "Clearly, their future pivots on a single, unresolved issue: will the Dunmurry plant rise to the cause and start building the silver bullets John Z. intended? Or will the De Lorean become another Concorde—a technical marvel that turns out to be an economic disaster? Find out for sure in our next installment."

Sherman's closing remarks triggered a small furor in England. A British journalist working in New York read Sherman's story and did an article about Sherman's criticisms of the car for his newspaper in London. As De Lorean PR Chief Mike Knepper remembers it, "My telephone rang from morning until night for two days," as English publications tried to use the *Car and Driver* article as proof of the Labour Party's folly.

For It's A Long, Long, Time . . .

The magazines would wait, of course, for their own U.S. road tests to *really* analyze the car, and they assumed that would happen soon after the press trip. It didn't. De Lorean was upset by the critical comments about the car's finish and quality and wanted to make very sure the test cars were correct. Bumper end caps weren't fitting the way they should, door striker plates didn't work as anticipated, and there were electrical and panel fit problems. As noted in Chapter 6, many of the early cars were getting a minor teardown in the Irvine facility so they could be put back together as expected. De Lorean was in a double-bind, because now that the cars were in production, the company needed them on the street, to get cash flowing

CAR AND DRIVER
Comparison Test Results:

	De Lorean	Porsche	Ferrari	Corvette	Datsun
0-60 mph (sec)	9.5	6.3	7.6	7.2	7.1
Top speed (mph)	120	135	140	130	135
Skidpad (g)	0.77	0.77	0.80	0.79	0.76
1000-ft slalom (mph)	55.1	58.5	55.6	58.5	56.7
Noise @ 70 mph (dBA)	75	76	83	76	72
Fuel economy (mpg)	18	17	13	15	15

(In this test, the skidpad is a 282-ft circle the car is driven around as fast as possible as one test of cornering ability. Noise is interior noise at a steady 70 mph.)

to the bank . . . and yet they couldn't rush so much that the cars would be unprepared for delivery.

May, June and July passed with no test cars available. Then one day Don Sherman called Knepper and quite bluntly told him that if they couldn't get a test car they were going to use a customer car and De Lorean would have to take its chances. Shortly thereafter the test cars became available.

Car and Driver Comparison Test Report

Car and Driver decided to test their De Lorean ($25,600) with four other cars: Porsche 911SC ($34,165), Ferrari 308GTSi ($56,650), Datsun 280-ZX Turbo (est. $17,500) and Chevrolet Corvette ($19,000). After their usual track test for the numbers, they would drive the cars on both public roads and at the Waterford Hills road racing course near their Ann Arbor, Michigan office. Things got off to a slow start when their first test 911 was rolled at Waterford by a non-staff member before the testing actually began.

If John De Lorean wasn't too happy with the original tests, he must have been grinning now. Eight paragraphs into the story *C/D* stated, "It pleases us no end to announce that John Zachary De Lorean has no reason to mount a rescue attempt for his brainchild. De Lorean and his new factory have done quite a splendid job of producing his car from the ground up. The bugs it bears lie at the easy-to-eliminate end of the scale, and with 3,000 De Loreans—and counting—built by late summer, it is obvious that the car is now ready to account for itself." There wasn't much the *Car and Driver* staff didn't like about the De Lorean. The usual comment about the fingerprints, the bunker-like visibility, and the high center console were there, and they didn't like the radio reception, but that was about it.

On the race course and the open road the De Lorean was the slowest of the five. Then the gull-wing car was measured against the others in a subjective evaluation among the editors for powertrain, handling, ride, interior comfort, interior convenience, sex appeal and fun-to-drive. The De Lorean ranked, respectively, 5th, 5th, 2nd, 4th, 3rd, 1st and tied for 4th.

As for the question of the De Lorean's handling at Waterford Hills with that rear-engine weight bias, *Car and Driver* said, "The De Lorean was hampered partly by its Corvairish tendency for the tail to make mild, unwanted advances toward passing its front at awkward times, but more by its simple lack of power. It is not gutless on the road, but neither does it bend your comprehension of acceleration."

It wouldn't appear from the numbers that the De Lorean would fare too well in the end, but it did. As the article's author, Larry Griffin, put it, "But you should not be concerned for the De Lorean. Yes, it was the slowest in Ohio [the open road portion—Ed.], just as it was in most of the proving-ground tests and at Waterford Hills, but then it's got tall gearing, excess curb weight, and the weakest engine. And the best fuel economy." He went on to mention the De Lorean Turbo and then the present car's tendency to ". . . get antsy indeed at hyperspeed over bad pavement . . .", suspecting it might have something to do with a lack of torsional stiffness in the car. (The De Lorean's torsional stiffness—the effort it would take to pick up a car at both ends and twist it—is lower than that of many cars.) He wraps the question up, however, by considering who the car is meant to please: "But such things need not concern California executives and similar breeds, because John's De Lorean will provide them with all the flash and substance they need. . . . What De Lorean has here is no less than *the* executive sports car."

Car and Driver's *acceleration test of the De Lorean with their "5th wheel" mounted with a suction cup.* (Aaron Kiley)

Road & Track Solo Test Report

Road & Track gave the De Lorean a solo test. As with *Car and Driver* they left no doubt in the reader's mind what the result of the test was, stating in the second paragraph, "De Lorean promised that he would build a distinctive, unusual and pleasant-driving GT when he embarked on this course in 1974, and while it took longer than he expected, he accomplished what he set out to do. It's a professionally designed and built car in every way, and has none of the kit-car feel that many critics expected."

Perhaps the most difficult road test to write is one in which the numbers gotten in testing the cars don't really fit with the subjective impressions. This problem is particularly tough in dealing with sports and GT cars because readers are so sensitive to test figures, even if they will never take a car to its limits of acceleration and handling. What matters most, however, is how the car feels as a total package—styling, fit and finish, comfort, acceleration, handling, ride, etc.—and not just the numbers.

As usual, *R&T*'s approach to the road test was more conservative than their Michigan counterpart's, taken from a traditionalist point of view. They found the styling ". . . handsome and uncommon," adding that the gullwing doors and stainless steel may fall into the gimmick category, but impracticality is not a vice in some cars, "especially in the $25,000-plus GT segment." After they commented that the stainless can look ". . . a bit shabby" if not kept clean, *R&T* added, "But the body pieces on our test car were well made and the fit was good, with all of the joints and interstices matching closely."

Inside the De Lorean they liked the use of leather, the driving position (". . . reasonably comfortable and there is sufficient adjustment of seat and steering wheel to suit most body types"), the driver's controls (". . . easily within reach and well marked for easy

understanding on short acquaintance") and the air-conditioning and ventilation system (". . . well thought out and works efficiently, providing lots of refrigerated air when called for—and that will be often, given the black interior and the miniscule toll-paying windows").

On The Other Hand . . .

On the other side of the question, *R&T* wasn't as impressed by the limited outward vision (". . . one area that comes in for criticism by most everyone who drives the car"), the seats (". . . shallow and skimpy on bolstering for the driver who is going to put the car through its ultimate paces, but for normal driving they are comfortable"), steering wheel position (". . . a touch too low for some tastes, despite its capacity for vertical adjustment . . ."), and the center console (". . . is slightly higher than most drivers would like and it adds to the sensation of being surrounded. It can also interfere with shifting . . .").

Their description of the general interior environment covered both ends of the scale: "There is very much an aircraft feel to being behind the wheel of the De Lorean, as the driving position is really a cockpit that envelopes the driver and either gives a feeling of claustrophobia or oneness with the car, depending on your personal proclivity."

Road & Track got their 5-speed De Lorean to 60 mph in 10.5 seconds, commenting that the car ". . . is not a barn-burner," but adding that is equivalent to the acceleration figures they've gotten on Jaguar's XJ-6, Porsche's 924 and Alfa Romeo's Spider Veloce and that ". . . the engine's flexibility makes up for its lack of brute horsepower."

As for driving the De Lorean, they thought the steering felt rather heavy initially, probably due to the large tires, ". . . but all combine to give a very good idea of what's happening between the rubber and the

MOTOR TREND
Comparsion Test Results:

	De Lorean	Corvette	Merak	928	Mondial
0-60 (sec)	9.98	8.25	9.39	7.38	8.20
1/4-mile (sec)	17.61	16.52	16.91	15.77	16.29
1/4-mile (mph)	77.40	83.80	83.80	85.80	84.50
Fuel economy (mpg)	26.8	19.3	19.1	20.6	17.1

road.'' As for the handling: "The basic handling characteristic is understeer, which can be modulated toward a neutral stance via a delicate throttle foot. Lift off the throttle in a corner and fairly high speed and the rear end tends to come around, as with most mid-engine or rear-engine cars. On their 100-ft skidpad, *R&T* got 0.772 g (similar to the Alfa Romeo GTV 6/2.5 and Ferrari Dino 308 GT4) and through their 700-ft slalom run the De Lorean hit 59.7 mph, just below the Porsche 924's 60.7 mph and above a Datsun 280ZX Turbo's 58.6 mph. "The rear-engine layout tends to produce a pendulum effect during the slalom runs if the driver goes too fast, resulting in the back end getting loose and out of shape." The car's braking distances were short, though the rears were sensitive to lock-up.

The result? "After adding up all the sums and reviewing our feelings, we're impressed with the De Lorean . . . it's quick enough to slice through traffic properly yet not so powerful that it will frighten the novice driver or burn a hole in your fuel bill. The ride is appropriately firm while still comfortable, and the handling is tidy and fun up to the car's uppermost limits, as long as the driver realizes that the rear weight bias results in handling that may be 'different' from what he's used to . . . John Z. De Lorean has reason to be proud: He's added a new dimension to the American sports car market.''

Motor Trend's Comparison Test Report

Hollywood-based *Motor Trend* decided on a group test, but with a somewhat different gathering than *C/D*. Instead of Porsche's 911 they chose the company's more expensive ($35,000 at the time of the test) 928. Ferrari's Mondial ($70,000), with its 2+2 seating, was chosen over the 2-only 308GTSi, which shares the same engine/gearbox. The Maserati Merak ($41,000) is just now out of production, but is in many

ways similar to the De Lorean, including Giugiaro styling. Like *C/D, Motor Trend* also included a Corvette with manual transmission ($18,671), feeling a test of the De Lorean without the all-American sports car would be incomplete.

The test began inauspiciously for the De Lorean, which had a broken alternator. Luckily (?) all five of the exotics were having (or would have) their problems before they were returned to their parent companies. *M/T* decided on a two-day trip throughout Southern California, because the make-up of the state allows a variety of road conditions to be sampled in 48 hours .

This magazine also had its own set of performance figures for the group in the test as shown in the Table.

There was also a voting system in which the various editors had a chance to give each of the five cars points in several areas: quality, styling, comfort, ride, handling, and engine response. The De Lorean placed respectively: 3rd, 3rd, 3rd, 3rd, 4th, and in a tie for 4th. Overall the Porsche had the highest score (130), the Ferrari was 2nd (113), the Maserati finished 3rd (83 points), with the De Lorean just behind (79 points) and the Corvette last (46 points).

As the official title of the trip was the Great De Lorean GT Value Lux-Out, the car did end up with a good score. In the Lux-Out Value Vote-Out, the editors gave the five cars points for their perceived dollar value. Once again the Porsche was on top, this time with 23 points, but the De Lorean was 2nd at 19 points, ahead of the Maserati (13 points), the Corvette (12 points) and the Ferrari (8 points).

At Speed With Ron Grable

Just as interesting as the voting at *Motor Trend* was a sidebar story on the car written by Ron Grable, an engineer and well known race driver. A man with a fine analytical touch at high speeds, Grable liked the idea of the De Lorean's X-shape backbone frame. He didn't like, however, the rear-engine placement, the 35 percent-front/65 percent-rear weight bias and the resulting high polar moment of inertia. As he explained the latter, "Inertia tends to keep it (the vehicle in motion) moving straight ahead, and any force—side wind, steering input, cornering loads—that tries to rotate it about its vertical axis must overcome this inertia. Thus, a vehicle with high polar moment of inertia is difficult to rotate or deviate from a straight line, but once it *is* rotating it is extremely difficult to stop." He then commented on the rear suspension and how the trailing arms allow the rear wheels to change their toe-in or toe-out (the inward or outward relation of the wheels to the direction of travel) as the car leans in a turn.

Grable then pointed out that these only come into effect at very high speeds, but added that the Ferrari and Maserati with mid- instead of rear-engine placement and unequal-length A-arm suspensions don't have these characteristics. As a result, he preferred the Italian pair's stability in high-speed (100–125 mph) corners. Grable also thought highly of the Porsche. "But the De Lorean's speed was restricted by its inherent high-speed cornering limitations—and the driver's white knuckles." After this he went on to add that the De Lorean's strong point was its braking, ". . . which was very linear and fade-free, with no pulling, squealing or lockup."

As Bill Collins and Mike Loasby explained throughout the car's development program, however, the De Lorean wasn't meant to be a race car, but a gentleman's sports car. From that standpoint Grable added, "It is an admirable 2-seat performance machine for people who like to travel by car, and I think its faults will be important only to a very few of its potential customers. Most people will find it an attractive, exciting, desirable piece with which to cruise the Beverly Hills Grand Prix—at a stately six-tenths."

"My God, It Was A New Company!"

In the end did John De Lorean feel he was treated fairly by the enthusiast press? "I think that generally speaking they were fair. Part of that was my own fault. I had inexperienced people in our PR department and I think we got the press in a little too early. You've got to remember we started a brand new factory with a completely untrained work force in a country that never built a car before. We had to assemble a strange management team who had never worked together or who did not know each other and we had to assemble them in an area that's a very difficult place to bring people because of the problems."

On the other hand, Bill Collins comments on the road tests by saying he felt the magazines were *very* fair with the De Lorean. C. R. "Dick" Brown agrees, adding, "They were very generous, though I think it's understandable . . . my God, it was a new company!"

Any automaker would like to wait until he had the perfect car before passing it on to the road testers . . . and several manufacturers pass their press cars back through the works in an attempt to do just that. In the end, De Lorean's criticism of his PR men —William Haddad and Mike Knepper—is unfair. Knepper in particular did what he could to fend off the press until "the car" was built, but there was just so long the magazines would wait before using an owner's car to test, thereby taking away what little control an automaker already has over such a test. Haddad, who didn't deal with the automotive press directly, left DMC in the autumn of 1981, amidst charges and countercharges between him and De Lorean about improprieties on both sides. Still more lawsuits were filed.

9

Coming Apart At The Seams

To OUTSIDE OBSERVERS, the first cracks in DMC's stainless armor began to appear in December, 1981—though like all stress cracks they were not ominous at first. Certainly De Lorean sales were down from their high of 720 in October, but in December virtually every automaker was in trouble in the U.S. Consumer spending was off, interest rates were still up and threatening to stay there, the weather in much of the country was terrible and, in general, it wasn't a time for buying such baubles as sports cars.

There was no reason to believe that January and February were going to be any better. Even the federal government was getting used to using the word "recession." Then, on January 5, De Lorean and the investment firm of Bache Halsey Stuart Shields withdrew for the second time a stock offering for a proposed parent of DMC to be called De Lorean Motors Holding Company. The first offering, in July, 1981 (intended to raise a total of $28,000,000), was dropped when Bache said it didn't feel the offering would be successful. The toned-down second attempt was meant to raise $12,000,000, again at $12 per share. In both cases, the capital was needed to buy out the De Lorean Research Partnership and begin development of the De Lorean sedan, which was the car everyone knew the company would need to sell if it was to be a long-term success.

There were, of course, good reasons for the lack of optimism on the part of potential investors in De Lorean. The company's inventory of new cars was now at the level where there was no point in trying to maintain high production levels. By the end of the year, 7,500 cars had been produced but only 3,000 sold. The painful decision was made to cut production back to a 3-day work week, while retaining all 2,600 employees. In those early weeks of January another problem snagged De Lorean, though it was a minor

blessing in disguise. Sea Link, the company that was responsible for the shipment of many De Lorean parts from England, was on strike, giving the factory another legitimate excuse to slow to the three-day work week and stop adding more cars to the rows of De Loreans already at the docks.

A Bridge Too Far

The ever-growing inventory of unsold De Loreans led to another problem that threatened the company. An important part of the financial structure of De Lorean Motor Company was something called bridge financing. This was a $34 million agreement with the Bank of America in California that, in essence, covered the cost of the cars from the time they left the factory in Northern Ireland until they were at the dealerships. However, the monthly interest costs of the bridge financing was high and, as automobile sales dropped and cars began to fill up the docks in Belfast and DMC's Quality Assurance Centers, the B of A loan wasn't enough to cover the increased number of cars between factory and dealerships. So, De Lorean went back to the British government for help, specifically to the Export Credit Guarantee Department (ECGD). It took the De Lorean presentation, requesting some $50-60 million, under advisement and the wait at DMC began.

Remember that the entire De Lorean deal had begun under the Labour government, promoted by Roy Mason, British M.P. for Northern Ireland. Now Margaret Thatcher's Conservative Party was in power and they were not inclined to automatically help the American entrepreneur. Two DMC previous requests for monies had been granted by her government because, to quote *The Sunday Times* of London, ". . .officials had advised that, Concorde-like, it would cost more to cancel than go ahead." The second batch of money came after what *The Sunday*

By summer, 1982, the QAC at Santa Ana, California, held more than 700 cars waiting for dealer orders that never came.
(Robin Riggs)

De Lorean Sedan

The 1980 Medusa, Giugiaro's lovely soft-edge four-door sedan—and De Lorean hope for the future. (Ital Design)

IT WAS APPARENT from the beginning that for DMC to be commercially successful the company would need to offer not just a sports car, but also a sedan. Even in the early design days of the sports car the possibility of carrying more than two people had been proposed. In fact, Ital Design produced two designs that stretched the present concept to handle a pair of rear seat passengers . . . who probably would have felt even more claustrophobic than those sitting up front.

Rather than a stretched concept, another Giorgetto Giugiaro design caught John De Lorean's imagination as a much more likely sedan his company could produce. Introduced at the Turin Auto Show in 1980, the Medusa is the perfect example of the sort of automobile the De Lorean sedan

should have been. The 2-door De Lorean sports car, particularly its stainless steel exterior, does hint of innovation, but underneath the car is rather conventional. The mid-engined Medusa could have provided that technological step forward . . . quite a feat for a 4-door sedan. One of the projections put the cost of that step, from design to production, at $80 million.

The Medusa is a very round and curvaceous design, pointing to a new period for Giugiaro, who has been a master of the hard edge. Not only is the Medusa very stylish despite its four doors, but with a drag coefficient measured at 0.263 in Fiat's wind tunnel, the car is very efficient aerodynamically. The mid-engine design is based on the Lancia Monte Carlo chassis, a car sold in the U.S. for

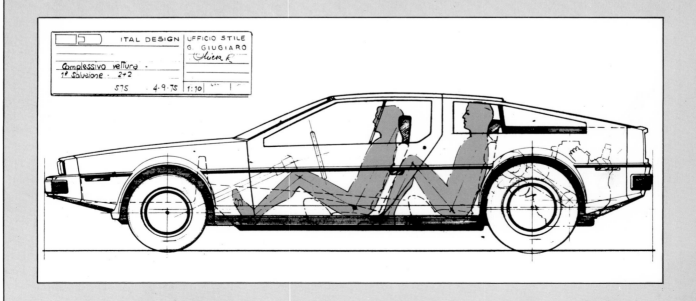

Bertone argued against four gullwings, did this 4-seat Marzal one-off for Lamborghini with two.

several years by Lancia as the Scorpion.

Inside, the Medusa is luxurious and conventional in many ways, particularly the seats and instrument panel. Yet there is also innovation, with all the necessary function switches grouped—somewhat confusingly, one suspects—in the center of the steering wheel. Think of it: A stainless steel-skinned Medusa with four gullwing doors. That would have been quite a sight.

Another car that caught De Lorean's eye was the Bertone-designed Lamborghini Marzal. When Bruce McWilliams went to the Turin Show in 1981, De Lorean asked him to visit Nuccio Bertone for advice on a gullwing sedan. The famous designer suggested against such a project, and brought up three basic objections. One was the high structural rigidity required for a vehicle in which you hollow out great holes that extend into the roof for the gullwing doors. You must then provide enough structure to support the door's weight. From that structure comes the second objection, for it would require an automobile that is quite heavy. Lastly, Bertone felt there was a real potential safety problem with these doors in a sedan. McWilliams added his personal objections to the doors, but De Lorean remained interested despite their feelings.

Trying to fit four passengers into his original De Lorean design, Giugiaro did a "stretched" version in September, 1975, but as you can see from this drawing, the two people in the back had to be very limber. Two other designs were also done, both similar to this one.

Times called, ". . . a notorious meeting at Stormont Castle . . ." and De Lorean was told that was ". . .the last handout." Nonetheless, he had to go back to the government for more when the introduction of the car was delayed, and this time the cash he received came in the form of government-guaranteed bank loans.

De Lorean says of that period and the months leading up to it as the fledgling company was getting started: "Remember, we were put in by the Labour government who made a tremendous amount of noise, publicity and everything else about our willingness to move into what was easily the most violent terrorist-ridden part of Belfast . . . so they made a big thing of it. Now when they were thrown out and the Conservatives got in we suddenly became the prize example of the extravagance of the previous administration. We were castigated and abused and kicked around by Parliament and then . . . the press got on our ass because it was an easy thing to do."

The Layoffs Begin

The British would argue that many of DMC's problems were self-made because instead of *trimming* production to suit the potentially stale winter months, De Lorean *doubled* production in November, thereby clogging the pipeline with unsold cars. On January 29 the British government turned down De Lorean's request. Faced with no solution to this crucial cash flow crunch, DMCL had no choice but to lay off 1,100 workers at the Dunmurry factory and cut production. In the U.S., some 200 De Lorean employees were cut adrift, many of them being workers at the company's three Quality Assurance Centers. These were the facilities set up to inspect the new De Loreans to make certain they were built correctly. Initially it was a long process, requiring 40-50 manhours per car, but as quality increased, the need for the QAC's had

(Far left) Laborite Roy Mason, MP for Northern Ireland, and (left) James Callaghan, then British Prime Minister, helped bring the De Lorean factory—and 2,600 jobs—to Belfast. Margaret Thatcher's Conservative government could not be persuaded to continue bailing with more finance, and hoped instead that private investment would carry the day. It didn't. (S & G Press Agency, Ltd.)

diminished. Word from DMC was that the closing of the QAC's had been part of the long-term plan, but the timing seemed too neat.

Next, the British government appointed Cork Gully, which is a member of Coopers & Lybrand, a noted accounting firm, to examine the financial state of the De Lorean project and determine what the chances were for saving the firm. (As an aside, Cork Gully has the wonderful address of Abacus House, Gutter Lane, Cheapside, London.) The diagnosis was bad, and on February 19, De Lorean Motor Cars Limited was placed under receivership.

This was similar to an American firm declaring Chapter 11 and trying to restructure the company's finances to the satisfaction of the creditors in hopes of making it work again. Now "Joint Receivers and Managers Appointed 19 February 1982" was typed ingloriously next to the nicely printed De Lorean letterhead on papers that came from the factory. Things looked dismal, but De Lorean, who was now becoming renowned for his psychological bouyancy under pressure, wasn't about to give up.

The Joint Receivers agreed to continue limited production of the sports car for five to six weeks in hopes that DMC could resolve its problems with the Bank of America, which was naturally alarmed when a company that had used up a $34 million line of B of A's credit was declared insolvent. John De Lorean said he had an investor interested in saving the company by buying the manufacturing facility from the British, the cost of the ante varying between $70-95 million depending on the source of the figures.

Advertisements offering De Loreans "Priced for Immediate Clearance (to make room for the new more expensive 1982's)" began to appear, hoping to create a little action in the showrooms. For DMC, however, the action was closer to home. On Monday, March 1, a further cutback took place within DMC and another wave of De Lorean employees went to work one morning only to go home jobless that night.

Faceoff At The QAC

In charge on the West Coast was C.R. "Dick" Brown, the man who had been so instrumental in raising the money for DMC. In December, Brown had been made the head of De Lorean Motor Cars of America, a company established to market the cars in the U.S. This new branch of DMC had come on the heels of the resignation of Eugene Cafiero, the ex-President and Chief Operating Officer of Chrysler who had been with DMC since 1979. However, disagreements between Brown and De Lorean had been intensifying for some time, and they now came to a head that first week in March. The pair "agreed to disagree," and De Lorean felt Brown should resign. Brown called the Bank of America to tell them about this latest change, he having been the one who arranged the bridge financing from that bank after several attempts to do so in the East had failed. On Thursday the bank called in the loan—and all hell broke loose.

At the QACs on both the East Coast at Bridgewater, Conn., and in the West in Santa Ana, Calif., control of the cars, by mutual consent between De Lorean and the Bank of America, was by a security company called Pasha Services. This was the bank's way of maintaining inventory control over the cars, which obviously were collateral for their loan. On Thursday evening a group of armed men representing themselves as being from De Lorean went to the Bridgewater QAC. After a loud squabble with the Pasha guards that eventually brought the police, 15 of the cars were driven to De Lorean's estate in New Jersey.

Brown, who was still at the De Lorean offices near the Santa Ana QAC, got wind that a similar move was going to be made there. Sure enough some

Bruce McWilliams, Director of Marketing for DMC and elevated to C.R. "Dick" Brown's post when the latter was fired March 5. He resigned after the British closed the factory on May 31.
(Dorothy Clendenin)

armed men did show up, but this time the police had been called ahead of time, and though a headline-grabbing argument ensued (Brown said the lives of he and his family were threatened if he didn't cooperate) all the cars stayed put. On Friday, March 5, C.R. Brown left De Lorean Motor Cars. This time he'd been telephonically fired by John Z. De Lorean.

Lawsuits And More Departures

The lawsuits began. On March 9, Bank of America got a court injunction to prevent the sale of any De Lorean car and to recover the 15 cars on John De Lorean's estate, which were returned. They also sued DMC to gain possession of 1,979 De Loreans they said were the collateral for the $17.6 million of principle and $380,000 of interest owed them. DMC, on the other hand, claimed it was not in default on the loan.

On April 7, Brown sued DMC for breach of his 5-year employment contract, which was to run through May 31, 1983. He was asking for damages of $260,166.23, and a trial date of April 29 was set (which, as it happened, was the same time Mike Loasby, De Lorean's Chief Engineer, quit in England). The judge issued a temporary restraining order against DMC selling or moving any cars until the case was settled. The case, however, never went to trial, ending instead in an out-of-court settlement. (As an interesting aside, listed in the suit among the assets of DMC, Santa Ana, was a 1955 Mercedes-Benz 300SL with, you guessed it, gullwing doors.)

While all this courtroom action was taking place, another important character had moved to center stage. Officially, Bruce McWilliams was the Marketing Vice President of De Lorean Motor Company, but now he became the acting president of DMCA, replacing Brown. McWilliams was a contrast to the flamboyant Brown. The latter, a Detroit native, had gone from American Motors Canada to Mazda in 1970 and, with

great fanfare, moved the Japanese company up the import car charts until the fuel crisis made the Mazda Wankel engine suspect on fuel economy and sales suffered dramatically. Outspoken and, by all appearances, tough to work for, Brown is nonetheless highly respected by many of his employees for his honesty and sincerity. When he left DMC, Brown plus Wendy Scheerer, his secretary and administrative assistant at DMC, and Kenneth Gorf, who has been in the financial department at the company, set up an office not far from DMC to help other former employees find new jobs. "I know people who jeopardized their family relationships to make this company (DMC) go," Brown comments, "people who worked literally 24 hours a day without stopping, and you just can't walk away from people like that."

Indigestion And Nausea

C.R. "Dick" Brown very simply wraps up what went wrong with DMC by saying, "It was, I think, that the style and appetite for growth was larger than the company's ability to digest and thus set in indigestion, dizziness, loss of equilibrium and some nausea. And that's what happened. For example, we increased production from 40 cars a day to 80 in November before we had justification for that on the retail market. And then with all the bad press, the flap between John and the British, everything came out in late December and January and depressed the retail market further and so we really couldn't sell what was being produced . . . and it went beyond the credit lines and they ended up shipping 1,100-1,200 cars that we couldn't pay for . . . those are cars worth $24 million and that absorbed all the working capital of De Lorean Motor Cars Limited and that threw them into receivership."

McWilliams now turned all his efforts to try to help save DMC. Soft-spoken and very much the East

Coast-style marketing man, McWilliams helped start Saab in the U.S. in the Fifties, then went to Mercedes-Benz before becoming the president in America of Rover automobiles. When that company became involved in a series of mergers that eventually made it a part of British Leyland, McWilliams stayed on and ended up in charge of marketing until late 1980, when he went to work for De Lorean as Marketing Vice President. Now, however, he wasn't trying to merchandise the product, but save the company.

Throughout this entire post-January 29 period, John Z. De Lorean had been looking for a financial savior for his company. In fact, it seemed as though De Lorean was constantly promising a person or company who would put up the money to save DMC was just days away from signing. The English magazine, *The Economist* would later comment, "Mr. De Lorean has found potential (and unnamed) buyers before."

There were potential saviors we knew about. Budget Rent-A-Car stepped forward with a plan to buy 1,000 De Loreans it would rent for $60 a day. The idea was that Budget would buy 1,000 cars from De Lorean dealers in late spring, use them for rentals in 30 cities around the country, and then sell them back to the dealers in the fall.

McWilliams had doubts about the Budget Rent-A-Car deal on three grounds. One was that because of DMC's financial condition the cars for Budget would have to be bought by local dealers, which would mean individual contracts between the company, the dealers and Budget . . . a paperwork nightmare. Secondly, the cars would go out of service in the fall of 1982, dumping 1,000 used De Loreans on the market. That had a good side in that it would open a new strata of owners who couldn't afford a new De Lorean, but that number of cars could also clog the market and dampen new car sales at a time then the company would need those higher-profit sales.

Lastly, the rental De Loreans would put a great number of potential owners behind the wheel for a few days and that held open the possibility of more sales. But if the cars deteriorated as many cars do under the rigors of rental drivers, it could also damage the gullwing coupe's reputation.

Sol Shenk To The Rescue

The other major plan, and the one that went through, involved a company called Consolidated International, Inc. Consolidated is known mainly for its ability to step into almost any situation where there are leftover vehicles that need to be sold somewhere. Remnants of Bricklin were one of the company's well known buys, but there were the 5,684 white elephant Fiats and Lancias that Consolidated bought for $55 million cash. The cars the Columbus, Ohio, firm couldn't sell to Fiat dealers were exported to Mexico, Peru and even as far as Egypt. Add in the assets of the Diamond Reo truck company Consolidated bought in 1975 for just over $11 million. Or a near $15 million paid for 333 Fiat-Allis bulldozers.

This $40 million-per-year, Dun & Bradstreet A1-rated firm is run by 71-year-old Sol Shenk. Go back to Shenk's beginnings and there seem to be a number of parallels between him and John De Lorean. Both are the product of large midwestern cities and experienced family lives that were disrupted when they were in their late teens. While De Lorean's parents were divorced, Shenk's died when he was just beginning college. Shenk and his brother and sisters were taken in by an uncle, who taught the young man the auto parts business.

There the Shenk/De Lorean parallel ends. During the Fifties and early Sixties, De Lorean was quickly climbing within the structure of General Motors. Shenk was on his own, trying to make an army surplus and an auto parts business work. When De Lorean reached

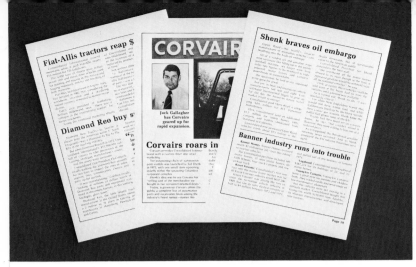

his peak in the mid-Sixties, Shenk was at the bottom, sorting out his business affairs with his creditors in court. In the early Seventies, De Lorean made his exit from GM, stepped into new executive offices and began creating new businesses. Shenk was also on the rise, but doing so by disassembling companies that had failed, selling off the assets or buying and selling huge stock surpluses. When the De Lorean Sports Car went into production in 1981, John Z. De Lorean had created a company with a debt (temporarily, it was hoped) of around $100 million, while Sol Shenk had developed one with $100 million of credit a mere phone call away.

Doing The Deal

Peter D. Franklin, writing in *The Columbus Dispatch*, outlines the first contacts between Consolidated and De Lorean in April, 1982: "Shenk worked fast . . . when he heard De Lorean was looking for an angel. 'De Lorean faced default on a $33 million loan from the BankAmerican Corp.,' said Shenk, 'so I called him up.'"

"He said, 'Come on in (to New York). You're the guy we're looking for.'"

Within hours Shenk was sitting in De Lorean's "triple first-class" office. For nearly two days they discussed the ins-and-outs of a deal. Shenk remembers De Lorean as "a very quiet man . . . his power structure was folding up." He also noted that De Lorean "was not a financial wizard."

Initially, Consolidated bought 1,174 De Loreans for $12,500 each, and 200 more De Loreans a few weeks later. That $17,175,000 went to pay off much of the almost $20,000,000 owed Bank of America. If DMC was successful later, it would buy the cars back from Consolidated for $13,500, and if DMC failed—and at this point some reports claimed bankruptcy papers already existed—then Consolidated would find

itself in the De Lorean business.

While the Consolidated deal wasn't a savior, at least it provided some breathing room. The Bank of America's restraining order was lifted and De Loreans could now be shipped from the port to the QAC and from there to the dealerships, but, as always, there were still more problems. One was that Consolidated, which held the paperwork on their 1,200 cars, wouldn't release any car and its paperwork until they had a check for the car . . . perhaps understandable considering Consolidated's stake, but a Catch-22 for cash-starved DMC. It was certainly an unusual system for the De Lorean dealers, who usually don't pay in advance. Adding to their reluctance to do this was the fact that many were owed something in the area of $1 million in warranty claims that DMC had not paid. There was another large sum owed dealers for financing floorplan money, which is a means of helping the dealer underwrite his cars between the time he receives them and when they are delivered to customers.

Scrapping For Survival

McWilliams was at this point working 14 hours a day, 7 days a week without pay, a situation many top executives at De Lorean shared as they scrapped for the company's survival. McWilliams now had a new plan. Under this proposal, DMC would offer the cars to the dealers at the same discount rate they had planned to offer Budget Rent-A-Car. There was also a built-in method of lowering De Lorean's debt to the dealers in the proposal. John De Lorean hesitated for a week, but then on Tuesday, April 13, he agreed to try it.

Telegrams were sent to all De Lorean dealers asking them to buy cars—four 1981 models and two 1982's—to help save the company. McWilliams reports that DMC received one reply from the 343 dealers. He said "No thanks." Undaunted, McWilliams and other DMC executives began an extensive telephone campaign to sell De Loreans.

McWilliams' idea was to let dealers buy cars at a discount, and at the same time whittle away at the money they were owed for warranty claims and floor-plan money. DMC would simply subtract from the invoice for the six new cars ordered the money DMC owed the dealer. This wouldn't work in all cases, of course, because there were instances when the dealer was owed *more* than could be covered by the number of cars he bought . . . or perhaps the dealer didn't *want* any new De Loreans. In other cases, once they subtracted the money owed the Bank of America plus the amount owed to a dealership the resulting balance was on the *debit* side of the ledger. Nonetheless, the mechanism was in place to begin moving cars from DMC to dealers and start struggling back from the debt that was staggering the automaker.

As you might expect, not every De Lorean dealer was actually working all that hard at selling the gull-wing cars. Four of the dealers had gone out of business and for many of the others, as one De Lorean executive put it, "We were 5 percent of their business and 95 percent of their problems." By May 3, the day shipments from the De Lorean Quality Assurance Center began anew, the company had orders for around 600 cars, less than two per dealer. With a little luck, plus the discounted price, plus a more positive image of the De Lorean company coming from increased sales, plus that annual sales gimmick—spring weather—maybe the company could clean out the QAC's and, eventually, order more cars from Northern Ireland.

A Little Trouble With The Water Bill

But—there were more problems. Of the 435 cars left on the docks at the Long Beach, California, harbor (the others had already been at the QAC's), half had suffered corrosion damage. The sea air's corrosive effects didn't get to the stainless steel or the epoxy-coated frame, but it did deteriorate little things such as nuts and bolts, driveshafts and alternator elements. McWilliams estimated it would take 40 man hours to clean the rust off from beneath some of the cars. He explained how such things were hurting DMC by adding, ". . . that was the kind of problem that if the company was strong and viable you'd think, 'Here's a few hundred grand to fix that problem,' but it's a low blow when we were having trouble paying the City of Irvine $300 for the water bill."

This discounting of De Loreans in May also caused a potential major problem to appear on the horizon of autumn, so to speak. Once you've sold De Loreans at a lower price to this new strata of buyers, how do you then increase the price on the next influx of cars from $19,999 to $28,000? McWilliams, ever the optimist, cited Jaguar's XJ6 sedan as an example that such a maneuver was possible. Sales of this car rose dramatically for the 1982 models not because the product had changed, but because public perception of it had, partially on the basis of a new 5-year/50,000-mile warranty. There would have to be more De Lorean interior color options and, at last, exterior colors. If things went very smoothly the Turbo De Lorean could also be considered again . . . if.

The level of optimism began to rise at DMC. Transporters loaded with De Loreans still sporting their styrofoam protective pieces from the factory were moving the cars from the ports to the Quality Assurance Centers in California and New Jersey. Every time DMC sold a car a large percentage of their margin had to go to the Bank of America to make up the difference between what Consolidated had paid and the money still owed the B of A. So the money coming in was going right out again, but at least the momentum was basically forward.

New York real estate tycoon Peter Kalikow had a taste of the car game in 1971 when he helped get this Momo Mirage built, but he couldn't come to terms with the British receivers and bowed out as a potential De Lorean savior. (Pete Coltrin)

Searching For Investors

And John De Lorean claimed to be near an agreement with a backer who would lift that weight permanently. Unfortunately, De Lorean couldn't (or wouldn't) name who his backer(s) was (were) and that just added to the cynicism, particularly in England. Fundamentally the plan called for DMC and The Savior to reacquire the Northern Ireland factory from the British receivers. Just who would provide the money? At one point it was said to be a group of real estate people from the East Coast, and then it was a West Coast financial consortium. Peter Kalikow, a real estate executive from New York who once backed a company that was to build a lovely car called the Momo Mirage, came close to being The Man Who Saved The De Lorean, but couldn't come to terms with the British receivers. John De Lorean and other DMC executives were in a constant search for these backers. McWilliams says that at one point he approached an Iranian multi-millionaire with the idea of saving the factory and putting his name on the car . . . just as Emil Jellinek underwrote Gottlieb Daimler's auto company and was able to name the automobile after his daughter, Mercedes. However, the lure wasn't enough and though the Iranian investor was interested, he bowed out.

The tab to underwrite the revival of DMC was about $35-40 million. At this point some 1,300 workers remained on the line at the Belfast factory producing 35-40 cars a week, which were then being added to the number already at the city's docks. So as De Lorean worked at putting together a group that would come forward to buy the factory and satisfy the British government that their $160 million investment still had some hope, at least the factory was open and equipment was being used.

Near the end of May, however, things began to fall apart again for DMC. The receivers announced that as of May 31 the factory was going to have to close. The week before, the remaining 1,300 workers were laid off, with only a skeleton crew of around 150 kept on to keep the factory from going to seed. Some 30-50 workers began to quietly occupy the plant on rotating shifts to protest the closure. Alan Watson Jr., of the *Belfast Telegraph,* explained their actions: "They haven't done anything that could be described as hysterical. They haven't taken any real militant action. Their hope is to either persuade the government to bring more money into the project or to persuade the government at the end of the day to pay them some form of compensation for the loss of their jobs. With the company in receivership and no cash, there's no money by way of compensation for redundancy or anything like that."

On the subject of John De Lorean he added that the workers had been somewhat upset about some things De Lorean said about Belfast: "I think it was a fairly emotional outburst on his part at the time, and it generally turned the workforce against him. They felt that he didn't give them enough credit for the work they put into it. They haven't seen him since the start of this year when things started to go sour. So they feel they are at least owed an explanation by him as to why the thing went so wrong."

Then Watson added, "There's also a school of thought among the union representatives that despite all these problems they've had with John De Lorean he is still very, very necessary for any attempt to rescue the place. And they've got a fair point. It's the man's car and his name is attached to it and he has a fairly solid hold on the U.S. company that is involved . . . John De Lorean will have to be a very senior figure in the operation. The British government doesn't want that and they'd rather see John De Lorean stay in the United States for the rest of his life. They're pretty sick of his name."

Don Lander, last man to sit in the California hot seat at DMC, formerly in charge of the factory in Northern Ireland. (DMC)

McWilliams Quits And Opines

When the receivers prepared to close the factory in Northern Ireland, in the U.S., Bruce McWilliams finally tossed in the towel and resigned, saying afterwards, "The burden of debt in the company is so staggering and with the receiver deciding to close the factory I really felt that was the kiss of death."

McWilliams' spot in the De Lorean's California hot seat was now taken by Don Lander. Before joining DMC in 1980, Lander had been the President and Chief Executive Officer of Chrysler Canada Ltd., which was just the latest in a line of top executive spots he'd filled for Chrysler through the world. He moved to the office in Irvine from Northern Ireland, where he had been in charge of DMCL, the arm of the company that actually built the cars.

After Bruce McWilliams left the De Lorean Motor Company he had several strong opinions about what went wrong. First was the car itself: "I think the product is not relative, is not good enough. Let me qualify that by saying that the car has good things in it and was assembled by people with care and dedication . . . but fundamentally I think the car is uninteresting, time just passed it by . . . it might have been great in the early Seventies, but it just isn't particularly interesting anymore.

"And functionally, in a design sense, it's really awful because the visibility situation is just thoroughly unacceptable. The small side window arrangement, which is a detail, becomes a nightmare. Also, the car lacked the diversity of color presentation that is a fundamental necessity. . . it's just not possible to sell these expensive cars in one color that isn't very well finished. It lacks an ultimate pizzazz and elegance, and that's a hell of a problem for it as a product.

"The car could never be sold in the numbers De Lorean predicted . . . from the earliest times I thought the numbers were outrageous and, indeed, all the internal research in the company stated that they were outrageous. In fact, the whole company was pitched at a level that was not realistic and could not be sustained. In the same area, the two-headed aspect of the company was a nightmare. You had a corporate staff in New York, and you had Dick Brown in California. There was no rationale for having two headquarters at all.

"Lastly, I would say the selection of dealers was monstrous. You had 345 dealers and certainly not better than half of them had any comprehension of how to sell this car. When it began to wobble they let it drop like a lead balloon.

"And the pity is that the whole damn thing was avoidable. It would be a totally viable company on modest sums."

Never Say Die

One might suspect that the closure of their factory would be the end of the De Lorean Motor Company, but it was not. John De Lorean went back to the receivers and arranged another plan that would restructure De Lorean Motor Cars Limited and put the factory back in business. Under this one, DMCL would be reorganized as "DMCL (1982)." The receivers would have until July 31 to develop a British consortium willing to take over the Belfast factory. If they did not, then De Lorean could win back the factory with a payment of $10 million in cash to get the facility operating once again and $25 million in export financing as a way of guaranteeing payment on the cars that would be shipped from Northern Ireland. As De Lorean explained the plan, not only would he then have the factory, but ". . . they wipe out all past obligations, all the debts are eliminated, all the supplier debts are eliminated, all royalty payments, everything is written off. Some $160 million worth of direct obligations and another $55 million

The confidence was slipping away. . . (DMC)

in redeemable preferred have all been eliminated, so the new company doesn't owe a cent.

"The suppliers have told this consortium under the government that all they want is the business to continue, because if we didn't continue, a number of the English companies would close because they couldn't exist with Jaguar alone. So they want us to continue to keep the company alive," De Lorean continued. And how can the British government just wipe out such a debt? ". . . because all the assets of the company in the U.K. (DMCL) are owned by and have always been owned by and are under a security agreement with the British government. They are the only secured creditor, so everything there belongs to them."

It seemed like an absolute sweetheart deal. The kicker was that De Lorean had to sell out the company's stocks of 1981 and 1982 cars before the British government would agree to the new plan and let DMCL (1982) start building 1983 models.

JZD Attacks The Credibility Gap

So what would convince buyers to take one of the leftover De Loreans? First was a new dealer discount, allowing them to profitably retail 1981 De Loreans for $19,999. Backing that would be a 5-year/50,000-mile warranty with the first 12-month or 12,000-mile portion secured by a major insurance company. And to get the message across to dealers and the public that the company was still alive and kicking, De Lorean made a mid-July trek through the U.S., telling dealers at meetings in San Francisco, Los Angeles, Dallas, Atlanta, Chicago, New York and Orlando that the company was still alive. For two weeks CBS radio stations in 10 of the company's major markets ran ads telling the public the same story. According to several accounts, De Lorean was looking tired and, for perhaps the first time, less than confident.

"How do you convince people that you're back in business?" De Lorean asked rhetorically in July, 1982. "It's very, very difficult. I liken it to a guy with a social disease. Your doctor cures you and he gives you a certificate that says you no longer have herpes simplex, but if you took that out at a cocktail party you wouldn't get too many dates. How do you turn around now and convince everyone you're back? We decided the only way to do it is to just be back. You've got to slowly fight your way back into the market and you've got to slowly convince the world that you're here and that you're here to stay and you're alive."

Even if it had all worked out perfectly, if DMC had cleaned out their stocks and the factory began building 1983 models, what was different about the company that would allow it to survive? DMC claimed that the hard times had slimmed the company and its fixed costs dramatically, trimming the direct costs of building the car by some $2,850 and cutting the breakeven point from around 10,000 cars per year to just over 4,000 cars. Combined with a renewed confidence in the car, the new warranty and a continuing line of product improvements, the De Lorean could be revived.

All De Lorean needed was that savior or consortium of saviors that would provide the needed $35,000,000 or so. Unfortunately, John De Lorean's saviors had become as elusive and ethereal as Joseph McCarthy's Communists. The British couldn't come up with their consortium to take over the factory, and John De Lorean couldn't find the money either. And yet as summer, 1982, faded, hope was still held out that something might happen. It would have been easy for the British to say, "It's over, thank you," and lock the factory up for good, but they didn't. In hindsight, it's easy to say maybe they should have, but this dream was now made not just of stainless steel, but flesh and blood.

141

10

The Aftermath

MY WIFE AND I had been in Stuttgart, West Germany to do some work at Porsche and Mercedes-Benz when we heard about John De Lorean. We were on the autobahn, driving back to England, listening to the news on the BBC Overseas Service, and expecting another broadcast headlining the crucial talks between the United States and Euopean steel producers over the question of dumping steel exports in the U.S. The discussions were critical to the British Steel Corporation and it would take a dramatic news story to displace steel from the headlines. John De Lorean was it.

What we heard was actually a double story, covering both the arrest of De Lorean on charges of drug trafficking to raise money for DMC and the announced closure of the De Lorean factory in Northern Ireland. The fact both stories broke at the same time had some members of Parliament wondering if the British government knew ahead of time that De Lorean was about to be arrested. And there were suggestions in Parliament once again that the whole British government/ John De Lorean/Northern Ireland affair must be investigated immediately. When we finally arrived at the ferry in Calais, France for the short run across the channel to England, I had a chance to read the complete stories about the "De Lorean affair."

More Than Just Scandal

Understand, the English tend to love a good scandal, whether it's another spy uncovered deep in the bowels of their security system, their young Prince Andrew off "on holiday" with an R-rated movie starlet, or the slick American entrepreneur who got their government to fork over millions of pounds sterling to back his automobile. But the De Lorean affair also contained serious questions about how the British government should handle projects funded by public monies. Know too, the variety of English daily

newspapers runs from those displaying quiet dignity to others shouting indignities. The stories in these English publications were different than those in American papers. In the U.S. the details of De Lorean's arrest and the operation that led to it were of prime importance, followed by a history of the De Lorean Motor Company. The involvement of the British was usually handled briefly. In England the drug story almost seemed secondary to the political side of where the money went and where the fingers should be pointed. This was a particularly difficult exercise because both political parties, Labour and Conservative, had passed money on to De Lorean, though the Conservatives had been reluctant to do so. As one commentator in the highly respected newpaper, *The Times*, said of the mood in Parliament, "Everybody was undoubtedly angry about it. But there was no agreement about who should be angry with whom." He went on to say of the Labour Members, "It is not the subsidy that they object to. Subsidies are their version of cocaine. It is the fact that the subsidy went to an American, worse an American who seemed to enjoy a good time."

The Times led its October 21 issue with the standard Associated Press photo of De Lorean in handcuffs and ran the headline "De Lorean taken handcuffed to face drug charge." The story was half about the drug bust and half on the financial and political implications. By the next day, the story's lead headline was "Political clash looms over funding of De Lorean." The drug arrest had moved to page 8. Now the main story talked about the fact "the De Lorean affair took on all the trappings of a political scandal . . ." The concern was with the 350 trade creditors being owed some $80 million, the main one being Renault, which was out $17-18 million for engines and transmissions. Questions of the De Lorean/Lotus-via-GPD arrangements were being

The headlines in Los Angeles and London had a slightly different flavor when the news broke of De Lorean's arrest.

raised again, and mention was made of the U.S. IRS investigation of the De Lorean Research Partnership.

Buying Jobs With Public Money

The *Financial Times* also used the De Lorean story at the top of the front page on October 21, followed by stories on the history of DMC and the effect the closing of the factory would have on outside suppliers. It was estimated the failure of De Lorean Motor Cars Limited would mean some 20 companies with more than 2,000 employees might have to shut down. More to the point, in many ways, was the newspaper's October 22 editorial on De Lorean, the matter of public investment in private enterprise and what lessons could be learned from the failure. It said, "The real question is more difficult: what financial risks can governments legitimately run when confronting problems as urgent and deep-seated as those in Northern Ireland? In our view the problems are so great as to justify some unorthodox risk-taking." After mentioning the various factors that caused the collapse of DMC, the *Financial Times* points out, "Venture capital is a rough, high-risk, ill-disciplined market," suggesting the risks should be spread out and "the more eggs they have in the same basket, the more closely the basket needs to be watched—particularly

where the entrepreneur has interests which may conflict with their own." After suggesting the government may have been ill-equipped to watch over a project such as the De Lorean, the editorial ends, "The whole tale serves precisely to demonstrate how difficult it is to buy jobs with public money."

(Remember that perhaps the ultimate indignity to the British public as far as the De Lorean Sports Car was concerned, was that despite all their investment in the car, they couldn't buy one. The right-hand drive version necessary for their market would have come in autumn, 1982.)

Tabloid Field Day

On the other end of the journalistic spectrum, one tabloid newspaper, the *Daily Star,* had John De Lorean sharing the front page with Princess Diana's early Christmas shopping spree. The headline read: "My High Life, By John De Lorean" and above his photo was the subhead "Star Picture Special On The Man Who Owes £100 Million." The lead story was so short its reading time was equivalent to a good sneeze. A story inside the paper on De Lorean's lifestyle was titled "Ritzy Road to Ruin."

Another tabloid, *The Sun*, had a 3-inch high headline that simply said "Chained" over the subhead

Newspaper treatment in England reflected the pent-up anger of many who had opposed the deal in the first place, feeling the money should have gone to an English firm, rather than De Lorean.

"Handcuffed De Lorean faces court," accompanied by photos of De Lorean and his wife, Cristina. The *Daily Mail* used the head "Scandal of De Lorean" accompanied by the line "Fury of MPs at Britain's wasted £81 million, 'It's monstrous . . . a devastating indictment.'" "De Lorean. MPs ask: Did he con us all the time?" queried the main headline in the *Daily Express*. The lead story contained the paragraph "Many Ministers [of Parliament—Ed.] who met De Lorean over the years and signed deals with him say he reminded them of J. R. Ewing of 'Dallas.'"

Those Americans not familiar with what happened to John De Lorean must number with those few who are uncertain of the identity of the President of the United States. On October 19, De Lorean was arrested in Room 501 of Los Angeles' Sheraton Plaza Hotel by FBI agents for his attempt to help finance a cocaine-selling operation. The resulting funds were said to have been meant to help bail-out the De Lorean Motor Company. In *Time* magazine, De Lorean is reported to have said of the bags of cocaine, "It's as good as gold and just in the nick of time."

In the end there were 11 counts to the indictment that alleged De Lorean, William Morgan Hetrick and Stephen Arrington had conspired to import some $5 million worth of cocaine into the U.S., where it could be sold on the street for around $50 million. The FBI claimed De Lorean was to put up $1.8 million while a man named Vicenza (actually an FBI undercover agent) would add the additional $3.2 million. For his efforts, Vicenza would get 50 percent of the De Lorean Motor Company. At last we found out who had risen to the top of De Lorean's potential savior list . . . though some ex-De Lorean executives question whether the money really was meant for DMC, because the financial connection would have been too close for public scrutiny.

No Place To Hide

The same 6-foot, 4-inch height that made De Lorean so imposing in the past was against him now. Television video tapes of the one-time GM executive walking to the van that would transport him from the Terminal Island Federal Correctional Institution near Los Angeles to various court dates had De Lorean towering over other prisoners. Even when tossled, the man's expensive haircut looked right, and it was obvious his rumpled shirt had a cut that was superior to the others'. The picture might even remind one of a scene from *A Tale of Two Cities* as the rich and poor walked together to the guilloutine. For John De Lorean it certainly was the worst of times. His bail was set at $5 million, then upped to $10 million.

The De Lorean Motor Company was going down with its leader. DMC's plush Park Avenue offices—a symbol to many of the company's critics of the sort of extravagance that had kept DMC from succeeding—were closed. An October 25 memo from Thomas W. Kimmerly, DMC's counsel as well as a company vice president and member of the board, was posted at the firm's facilities. It read: "At approximately 3:15 today, De Lorean Motor Company filed, in Detroit, a Petition under Chapter 11 of the Federal Bankruptcy Act. The Petition has been assigned to Judge Woods and the case number is 82-06031." Four days later John De Lorean was released on bail that had been secured with several of De Lorean's real estate holdings.

As one might readily expect, John De Lorean was paying for all this in places other than the courts. De Lorean jokes were an instant hit, so to speak. "Do you know what the ultimate automotive status symbol is? A De Lorean with a license plate made by De Lorean." "The De Lorean is the only car that will cruise down the highway, sucking up the white lines as it goes." One dealer, Jepsen Chevrolet/De Lorean,

Sol Shenk. In total he bought 2,487 De Loreans. (Wide World)

Seen in Green Bay (Wisconsin) Press Gazette.

in Green Bay, Wisconsin, ran an ad that read, "Buy the De Lorean and get 60 lbs. of Coke," adding below that, "De Loreans go better with Coke!" The promotion promised that if you bought a De Lorean, the dealership would give you 60 pounds of Coca-Cola . . . a promotion that did not sit well with the soft drink firm.

Life In The Pressure Cooker

Many of the comments about John De Lorean weren't humorous. Former DMC executives hadn't said much about De Lorean in the past, but then there wasn't anyone really listening. As Robert Dewey, who was De Lorean's initial chief financial officer, put it, "In the eyes of so many, De Lorean was bigger-than-life. We would have been a voice in the wilderness. . . it would have sounded like sour grapes, and the press wouldn't have picked it up." When both Mike Knepper and Bruce McWilliams did stories about their experiences at DMC, De Lorean branded them as turncoats. Now several men who had been at the top in DMC came forward to describe life in that pressure cooker. There were stories of frustrated senior executives of the company who had been denied the chance to trade their DMC stock when De Lorean refused to register that stock. Then, when the stillborn De Lorean Motor Holding Company was proposed, this would have been the stock eligible for trade over the counter, while the employees' DMC stock couldn't. Others spoke vehemently about the shabby manner in which the British were treated by De Lorean despite the considerable stake that country had in his company. Dewey comments: "I saw him treat them [the British] almost as outsiders. If they asked questions they were irritating his master plan. He didn't feel accountable to the British." And former employees brought up a matter the British press had often questioned, that of company executives spending time on De Lorean's per-

sonal business projects.

All this was not the end of DMC. Chapter 11 is not meant as a final blow, but a means of giving a company time to arrange with its debtors to meet its obligations. At this point a name from the past reenters: Consolidated International of Columbus, Ohio. Remember that Consolidated had taken control of 1,391 De Loreans in April and May for a payment of some $17.4 million as a means to give DMC some financial breathing room. DMC still owed Consolidated almost $9 million. Now Consolidated was allowed to take control of the remaining 649 cars DMC had in the U.S., plus the inventory of parts and a good share of the company's furniture.

Thinking Big In Columbus

Consolidated's Chairman and President, Sol Shenk, who tends to think big in such situations, wasn't just trying to buy up the local inventory, because next his company also bought for $1.25 million the rights to sell the De Loreans that remained in Ireland, with an annual $50,000 payment to DMC. The Ohio company purchased the De Loreans that were overseas, including 1,041 that had been completed and 53 that were in the process of being built. Most of these cars were 1982 models, though there were some that had been converted to 1983's, plus 100 cars built to meet Canada's automotive regulations. The plan is to sell the cars through the present De Lorean dealer network. Shenk arranged for a 12-month/12,000-mile warranty for the De Loreans he would be selling.

At the same time, Consolidated picked up a 45-day option (expiring Jan. 1, 1983) to acquire a 99-year lease on the De Lorean factory. Shenk sent accountants to Belfast to see if the numbers would add up to save the De Lorean car.

Run an Irish automaker from Columbus, Ohio?

145

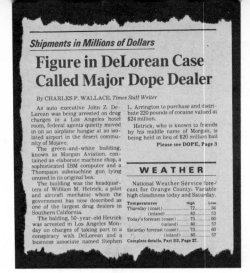

L.A. Times *told how De Lorean stepped into major FBI investigation*

Shipments in Millions of Dollars

Figure in DeLorean Case Called Major Dope Dealer

By CHARLES P. WALLACE, *Times Staff Writer*

As auto executive John Z. De-Lorean was being arrested on drug charges in a Los Angeles hotel room, federal agents quietly moved in on an airplane hangar at an isolated airport in the desert community of Mojave.

The green-and-white building, known as Morgan Aviation, contained an elaborate machine shop, a sophisticated IBM computer and a Thompson submachine gun lying unused in its original box.

The building was the headquarters of William M. Hetrick, a pilot and aircraft mechanic whom the government has now described as one of the largest drug dealers in Southern California.

The balding, 50-year-old Hetrick was arrested in Los Angeles Monday on charges of taking part in a conspiracy with DeLorean and a business associate named Stephen

L. Arrington to purchase and distribute 220 pounds of cocaine valued at $24 million.

Hetrick, who is known to friends by his middle name of Morgan, is being held in lieu of $20 million bail

Please see DOPE, Page 3

WEATHER

National Weather Service forecast for Orange County: Variable high cloudiness today and Saturday.

Temperatures	High	Low
Thursday (coast)	72	56
(inland)	82	52
Today's forecast (coast)	73	60
(inland)	80	57
Saturday forecast (coast)	73	60
(inland)	80	57

Complete details, Part III, Page 27.

London's Financial Times *of October 21.*

It all sounds very complicated. "That's not quite true," Shenk claims. "We engage in many businesses. We have an operation in Singapore, we have an operation in Texas, we have numerous operations around the country and many of them are just as complicated. We're very well versed and adapted to different situations . . . that wouldn't bother me. The only thing that would bother us would be the economics: Can we build the car there on a small volume economically enough to sell in the United States?"

"It's an excellent automobile," Shenk says of the De Lorean. "The car, in my opinion, compares very favorably with a Porsche, even a Ferrari. A very well-built car."

What would the future Shenk/De Lorean be like? "I would gradually shift the components to U.S. manufacturers. Unquestionably the car would have to be painted. The stainless steel was a mistake. It's much more expensive. With regular sheetmetal the car could be produced a couple of thousand dollars cheaper. You know, everybody wants a different color . . . and the stainless steel doesn't keep clean."

"I think it's a marvelous factory," Shenk says of the Northern Ireland facility. "Two things: One, he did not provide for painting the car. And that could be very expensive. He couldn't visualize that . . . a demand for painted cars. Secondly, of course, those four or five separate buildings . . . he should have gotten his sights down lower to start with."

That theme of beginning too big seems to run through Shenk's thoughts about John De Lorean: ". . . he set his sights too high. He was a General Motors man and I think he thought in terms of big volume. Instead of building 4,000–5,000 cars he set a goal of 30,000 cars . . . way too high." Shenk adds, "I think the car should sell for about $40,000–$50,000 and we would want to try to get that. If he'd come out with that car at $40,000 I think he would have sold

3,000–4,000 cars and it could have been a tremendous thing. Now you can't get the public to take that big a hike, and that's what it should sell for to take care of its production costs."

Shenk's instincts were subsequently backed up by his financial analysts, and on December 23, 1982, he announced Consolidated would not be exercising the option to continue building De Lorean Sports Cars. On December 24th the last De Lorean was constructed in Dunmurry, Northern Ireland, the same day creditors of DMC in the United States announced they would attempt to attach John De Lorean's personal assets to recover their losses.

Trying To Add Up The Numbers

While Consolidated still was poring over the numbers to see if the De Lorean could be built, the U.S. Internal Revenue Service was checking the numbers that got the De Lorean to production in the first place. There had always been rumors about what money went where, though most whispers were hushed when the De Lorean Sports Car made it to production. As DMC's problems grew, so once again did the questions. The link between John De Lorean and Lotus via General Products Development Services Inc. has been brought up to question. Just how much of the $17.6 million went directly to Lotus? And was the total really $17.6 million? The IRS also decided to closely audit the returns of the partners in the last investment group, the De Lorean Research Limited Partnership, because that money was supposed to go for research and development. Still more and more questions . . . which lead one to ask, when will it all end?

Neither quickly nor simply, one suspects.

There is one question, however, that needs an answer right now. What was it about John De Lorean and the promise of his company and its automobile that drove men such as Bill Collins, Robert Dewey,

146

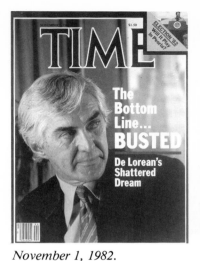

November 1, 1982.   *November 8, 1982.*   *November 29, 1982.*

C. R. Brown, Jerry Williamson, Don Lander and Bruce McWilliams (just to name a very few) to work the long, tireless hours they did? McWilliams explains: "I believed that it was important for the company to succeed and, indeed, it could have done so. As a personal endeavor, De Lorean's achievement in creating a car company went way beyond what anyone else had attempted for a long time. To try to make the enterprise work was worthy of one's best efforts. American enterprise needs a shot in the arm which the success of a new, small company could have provided. The free enterprise system in America is suffering from the symptoms of its own obesity.

"DMC had serious and tragically unnecessary flaws. However, one could never have said it was boring or deadly dull. It was often hair-raising, sometimes awesome, and always immensely alive. No one was just going through the motions—it was balls to the wall all the way. De Lorean confirmed that the realm of possibility is much greater than usually imagined. Regardless of subsequent events, a heroic dimension to De Lorean's efforts should not be forgotten.

"There are people prepared to stand on the sidelines and say that De Lorean should have done things differently, but the criticisms levelled by these all-knowing people are often not the ones that caused the enterprise to fail.

"Of course, Bricklin had a stab at building a car, but De Lorean had knowledge and skills of an altogether greater magnitude. Indeed, one of the central problems stemmed from long years of being accustomed to doing things in a manner and at a level far in excess of what a fledgling company could tolerate."

Unfortunately, as the De Lorean drama has been played out—soap opera-style with Cristina De Lorean's diary in *People* magazine, and in a hard news manner in the newspapers as the lawyers jockey for position—the original source of it all, the De Lorean

Sports Car (nee DMC-12, nee De Lorean-Allstate Safety Car), has been forgotten. It isn't a perfect automobile. Bruce McWilliams is probably right that it needed exterior colors right from the beginning. Black-only interiors at introduction was a mistake. C. R. Brown is correct when he says the car needed still more product development. The original system of larger, sliding windows was preferable to the small power windows. It would have been nice if the De Lorean were mid-engined and had more power.

Of all the imperfections noted, the most frustrating is Brown's comment about the lack of more complete development. Understand that expensive exotic cars are not always the most completely developed automobiles in the world. They have stunning exteriors and excellent engines and/or suspensions, but that image may hide problematical electrical systems, insufficient cooling and a body that will rust as soon (or sooner) than more mundane cars. The De Lorean was going to be different in this respect and it's significant that De Lorean considered having his car developed by a company that does fully develop its exotic cars: Porsche. But as the book *Project 928*, describing the development of the Porsche 928, points out, you need four years and at least $45 million to do that. Squeezed by time, De Lorean produced a good car, but not a great one . . . it needed a little more time to freeze into something solid.

This is, of course, the terribly practical side of things. If the shape of the De Lorean stirs you, and you find the gullwing doors fascinating and regardless of what anyone else thinks you find it damn exciting —buy it! That's why this genre of automobile exists. No doubt the De Lorean will be used for decades as a stern example why no man should ever try such a venture. Luckily, human nature being what it is, men will ignore the advice and try again. At least we hope so.

147

EPILOGUE:
The Knepper Chronicles

IN THE AFTERMATH of the De Lorean cocaine bust, few journalists spent much time writing anything good about the man. That's understandable. Writers and reporters, afterall, have to look to the demands of their readership, and when a hero falls that readership typically becomes a pack of voracious sharks in a feeding frenzy for more bad news, for the next tidbit to be thrown into the water. We like our heroes. We demand them. But there's a dark side to the collective American psyche. We also take a smug delight in the plight of fallen heroes. Not if the Fates have conspired against them. That's reason for clucking sympathy. But when a hero fells himself, the sharks circle. And maybe that's the way it should be. With hero status comes a responsibility. Heroes must act like heroes. They can't allow themselves to submit to the weaknesses that are part of the human condition, to simply make mistakes. If they do, the popular wisdom goes, they deserve everything they get and kicking them when they're down is accepted practice.

Despite his universal conviction in the popular press, as this is written De Lorean is innocent in the eyes of the law. But never mind. He's involved, and even if a court of law absolves him of all complicity in the drug thing, he's marked.

He understands. When the British government had given the De Lorean Motor Company a clean bill of health after the allegations of the misuse of public funds, he went directly on the offensive by slapping lawsuits on a couple of individuals and that bastion of Britishness, the BBC. The company had taken several body blows, and he wanted to throw some counter punches, to get his story into the press with the intensity the allegation stories had generated. Being absolved wasn't enough.

"It's like getting a piece of paper from your doctor saying you're not crazy," he once explained to me.

"You can show it all over town, but the damage has been done."

This time, however, I think too much damage has been done. I don't think a hundred lawsuits and all the other offensive tricks he might be able to stage can ever get him back what he once had.

It's too bad it had to end that way. The drug bust and whatever final lines it may ultimately add to the De Lorean saga will inevitably be what he's remembered for, what's most remembered about him.

I don't know if John De Lorean is a good man or a bad man. I know that in the 18 months I worked closely with him I found a lot to like and admire, but also a good bit about which I can be critical. I know little more than what has been written time and again in newspapers and magazines about his life and business activities before the De Lorean Motor Co. I left his employ in March, 1982, and similarly have no inside knowledge of the company's death throes that summer and the drug bust. But I was there for 18 exciting months, from just before the factory was completed until that final "No" from the British government. Although a full recounting of those 18 months would take another book this size, what follows are some observations from inside. **M. K.**

Up On The 43rd Floor

I met John De Lorean one August afternoon in 1980 in his 43rd floor office on Park Avenue in Manhattan. I was there for a job interview. De Lorean's Vice President for Corporate Development and Communication, Bill Haddad, had asked me to fly in from Ann Arbor where I was working for *Car and Driver* magazine to talk about becoming DMC's Director of Public Relations. John was particularly concerned about the company's relationships with the enthusiast publications and was looking for an expert in that area.

Living the nightmare, John De Lorean leaves Parker Center in Los Angeles on October 20 to face arraignment in Federal Court on drug trafficking charges. (Wide World)

You got to the 43rd floor via an express elevator that emptied you out in front of a pair of glass doors that in turn opened onto a huge, dimly lit cavernous reception area. There were low-slung leather chairs in facing pairs on either side of a central path to the receptionist. Sitting against the walls, one on each side, were representations of a man and a woman—statues? sculptures?—made of an assortment of, well, everything. Like a hardware store had exploded and the artist went through the rubble picking up a stainless steel fork here, a roll of wire there. And there were lots of automotive parts: sparkplugs, shock absorbers. Bizarre modern art. Impressive, too, which is a word that would easily apply to everything else I saw that afternoon.

Haddad came out to usher me into the office area. Through the door beside the receptionist you walked into another huge expanse, this one bright and sunny in contrast to the subdued lighting and dark appointments in the reception area. The floor was covered with gleaming white marble tile as slick and shiny as glass. And devoid of furniture or office equipment of any kind. Against the wall to the right and the left, secretaries sat behind bunker-like counters with a small built-in desk. Straight ahead the marble tile gave way to a carpeted area filled with smoked-glass partitioned offices with floor to ceiling windows looking out on the uptown Manhattan skyline. Impressive. De Lorean's office was down a tiled hallway to the right, past two well-appointed executive offices.

A Pretty Good Adrenalin Shiver

We paused at the open door to De Lorean's office. Over Haddad's shoulder I could see, what seemed like 100 feet away but was actually no more than 30, that familiar gray head bent over some work. Haddad said, "Mike Knepper's here," and De Lorean looked up, smiled and began to rise. And it seemed for a moment as if he would never stop unwinding from behind the desk. A couple of long strides and he was standing in front of me, hand stuck out, all sparkling teeth, silver hair, blue eyes, matching blue shirt, jutting chin. Impressive.

Over the years I've had the pleasure, or at least the experience, of meeting a lot of important/famous /legendary/people, (hell, I've even been to a backyard barbecue where Paul Newman was the chef; the burgers came off almost inedibly raw) so I'm no novice in that department. But take away the nervousness any prospective employee would have under those circumstances and I was still left with enough synapse activity to fire off a pretty good adrenalin shiver. Impressive.

During the next 18 months I would have many opportunities to recall that moment when I saw it repeated with visitors I took into De Lorean's office for their first meeting with the legend. It became easy to understand how dealers, private investors and the British government could so confidently hand over their millions when that "presence," all silver hair, blue eyes, matching blue shirt and jutting chin was sitting across the meeting table.

De Lorean's office was large and comfortable but far from the over-done luxury easy to find in Manhattan. It was furnished elegantly with a "conversation" area in one corner—a sofa and John's matching easy chair at right angles—with another matching sofa across the room against the wall. His desk was one of those drawer-less executive affairs—actually more a heavy table—in blond burled wood of some flavor. To his left as he sat, a section of the wall was covered with a hodge-podge of photographs of Cristina, John and the kids, including a four-color poster of John and his son, Zachary, on a rocky seashore. He had printed up and mailed the poster as a Christmas card one year. A brass telescope was set up against the windows. A sign hanging on it, part of an advertising

Eugene Cafiero, former President of Chrysler Corporation, who De Lorean hired to head DMC. He left in 1981, untainted by all that would follow. (DMC)

agency's attempt at getting the De Lorean business, said, "Pardon the delay in getting your new De Lorean. We're building them as slowly as we can." Pretty good, I always thought.

The Sumptuous Digs

The cumulative effect of the De Lorean Motor Co. offices was the portrayal of just what John intended: a successful business operation, important, he felt, in convincing the money people he was constantly courting that it was a good place to leave behind some investment dollars. Later, when we were begging money for our survival, it signaled quite a different message, especially to the British: profligate spending. But it must be pointed out that, typically, De Lorean had cut a deal for the offices. They had originally been the Exxon corporate biggie's offices and boardroom. De Lorean, through his contacts, had been able to sublet the space at a rate far, far below the going rate in Manhattan for such sumptuous digs.

I started work, moving into one of those smoked-glass enclosures, in September, 1980. It was an exciting time for DMC, and you could feel the tension, the air of anticipation of the great things to come. I remember being particularly impressed with the quality of the people De Lorean had gathered around himself. Curiously, with the exception of De Lorean and one other we'll get to in a moment, I was the only one of a staff of perhaps 20 professionals in the New York office with any automotive experience. That immediately cast me as the corporate font of automotive information. One VP, Buck Penrose, a brilliant, meticulous 40-year-old bachelor, seemed constantly up against a deadline to produce a revision of the corporate "plan" that spelled out everything from the makeup of the board of directors to the competition for the about-to-be born De Lorean car, and I spent hours, days pulling together information about that competition: road test results,

specifications, sales figures and such. And I discovered one of the major flaws in the marketing strategy De Lorean was selling potential investors.

Since the new car was by standard definition a sports car, it was incumbent upon the company to prove the sports car market was big enough to absorb 25,000 new De Loreans each year. Fair enough, but the logic went out the 43rd floor windows when Penrose, at De Lorean's direction I have to assume, tallied up the sports car market by including sales figures of every car with a "sporty" image: Honda Accord coupes, Dodge Chargers, every Camaro and Firebird, not even restricting it to Z28's and Trans-Am's. But including all those sporty cars made the figures say what the company wanted: the market was plenty big enough for us to play in.

Eugene Cafiero: A Class Act

There were some interesting players up there on the 43rd floor. Some permanent, some transient. Eugene Cafiero was our President. Cafiero was the other automotive type on the staff. He had most recently been the president of the Chrysler Corporation, but had been handed his head when the company went in the financial toilet and Iacocca loomed on the corporate horizon. His job was to "liaise," in

Haig-speak, between the manufacturing operation going up in N. Ireland and De Lorean in New York. But that included the very important job of making sure the manufacturing operation did indeed get put together. He had done that sort of thing on his way up the Chrysler ladder, so he was uniquely suited to the assignment. He was not so well suited to working as John De Lorean's right hand. The past-president of Chrysler felt he brought a certain amount of ability to the presidency of this "nickel-shit little company," as De Lorean liked to describe it, and logically assumed he should be left alone to get the job done. But the game was all De Lorean's. After all, his name was on it. Cafiero rankled under De Lorean's second-guessing method of operating, and being relegated to high-paid assistant status. After all, he had run a company— no judgment here on how well—that had a weekly payroll that was many times the entire value of the De Lorean operation.

Cafiero "resigned" late in 1981 to pursue other interests, having, as I recall the press release he dictated to me, "accomplished the task I had been hired to do" which was bringing the De Lorean into production. Unofficially and for internal explanation, he had failed to meet some half-dozen deadlines in the construction plant project, including the start up of production. But cutting through it all, I think it was simply a matter of Gene getting his fill of De Lorean. Or maybe De Lorean getting his fill of Gene. Whichever. I like Gene Cafiero and am pleased he was able to leave the company untainted by anything that had transpired—the memo scandal, allegations about the misuse of funds—or would transpire. He's a class act.

The Adventures of Bill Haddad

Any list of interesting players De Lorean brought in to the operation has to have Bill Haddad at the top.

Bill, an award-winning newspaper man, also counts in his past a long involvement with Democratic politics. More specifically, he was closely involved with the Kennedy administration where he was instrumental in helping Sargeant Shriver start up the Peace Corps. The walls of his office were covered with a most impressive array of autographed photographs from LBJ, JFK, Teddy Kennedy, Hubert Humphrey, Estes Kefauver, Jimmy Carter and a few others. Bill, to put it mildly, was well connected in Washington. And it was that direct connection with Washington De Lorean wanted, particularly where it could help further the cause of the DMC 80, a public transportation-type bus he wanted to build and sell. But more on that later.

What little public relations work had been done had been done by Bill. But in that regard Bill mostly answered requests for interviews with De Lorean, provided some facts and figures when reporters called, and little else. His main area of attention as far as DMC was concerned seemed to be getting the inside scoop on what the British government and journalists were thinking, might think, ought to think, would think and then writing John long, disjointed memos about the situation. Bill also had some secretive, undercover-type contacts he had presumably developed during his many years deep in the intrigues of national politics. Through those contacts Bill was able to get a steady supply of confidential information about the Irish Republican Army and its attitudes and planned actions regarding De Lorean Motor Cars Ltd. in Belfast. In fact, one evening Bill arranged to be taken to an apartment in Belfast where he met a hooded officer of the IRA. The purpose of the meeting was to find out what the IRA intended to do to the De Lorean plant. The answer, nothing. The jobs meant too much to jeopardize with terrorism.

In the recounting of that story, Bill showed just the right amount of remembered fear. But not much.

He was happiest when involved with an intrigue of some kind or another. He could sense a plot or conspiracy under every desk, behind every closed door. Too many years in politics will do that to you, I suppose. Still, in all those years he had developed a sixth sense for what was going on, for getting behind the obvious and revealing real motives. At least as he saw them.

Take the stock options situation that eventually led to Haddad's falling out with De Lorean. Simply stated, as an inducement to key people to leave positions of seniority and vested interest and join his new venture, De Lorean offered very appealing stock option plans. Executives would be able to buy stock in The De Lorean Motor Co. for ten cents a share that would someday, theoretically, be worth many, many times that. The unwritten understanding was that De Lorean would take DMC public. However, much to everyone's surprise, De Lorean did not try to take DMC public. Instead, he created an entirely new company, De Lorean Motors Holding Co., and planned to offer its shares to the public. That would have had the net effect of making the executives' DMC shares essentially valueless. De Lorean, by the way, would own a huge number of the new DLMH shares, the executives none.

"Some of our guys have their entire futures hooked to the eventual value of their DMC stock," Bill fumed. "You just don't do that to people."

As it turned out, after spending some $2 million dollars on lawyers, accountants and the huge costs of writing and printing all the necessary pre-issue documents, the De Lorean Motors Holding Co. plan was scuttled at the last minute, literally, when the underwriter told De Lorean that the offering would die unpurchased. And of course the DMC stock would eventually be worthless for an entirely different reason. But the rift between Haddad and De Lorean had grown too wide to repair. Their relationship is now in the legal limbo of suit and counter suit amounting to hundreds of millions of dollars.

The Great Memo Scandal

Haddad also played an interesting role in what may be the singularly most interesting De Lorean vignette of all. I call it The Great Memo Scandal. The key figure in the scandal was Marian Gibson. When I joined the company, Marian was the doyenne of the 43rd floor: De Lorean's personal and executive secretary. English by birth, Marian had lived in the U.S. for many years and had been with JZD about two years, maybe longer. Very officious, very helpful—perhaps too helpful, as sometime after I arrived John apparently created the job of office manager to get Marian out of *his* office.

Marian quickly expanded the office manager's job to fit her needs for authority and in the process managed to alienate just about everybody she hadn't managed to alienate in the old position. But Marian was loyal, the feeling seemed to run, so rather than simply dismiss her (it was later suggested De Lorean feared Marian "knew too much" about the operation) they decided to find her another slot. As fate would have it, the slot that needed filling was a secretary for me. The thinking was that Marian, having been De Lorean's personal secretary and then office manager, would feel demeaned by working for the lowly Director of Public Relations, and would quit. Although the "demotion" definitely had a most dramatic affect on Marian, her reaction wasn't exactly what De Lorean had hoped for.

Somewhere in all the messing about, Marian decided that not only was she getting a raw deal, but the British government had been and was getting more of the same. She collected large quantities of official DMC correspondence, including inter-office memos.

Nicholas Winterton, British M.P. (Maccelsfield) who took secretary Marion Gibson's charges public and ignited "The Great Memo Scandal." (S & G Press Agency, Ltd.)

Her task was simplified—in fact the entire idea may have occurred to her at this point—when she was asked to help clean out Haddad's office. His break with De Lorean over the stock situation had escalated to the point Bill knew he was a short-timer at DMC and he wanted his files, etc. moved to his apartment. Marian helped Bill's secretary box up and move out. Friday evening, October 2, 1981, Marian said, "Good night." I said, "See you Monday morning." Wrong.

Over the weekend, Marian flew to England with her box of goodies and handed them over to Nicholas Winterton, a Member of Parliament. And with the help of a New York-based British correspondent, took her story to the London tabloids. Right or wrong, truth or fantasy, Marian had determined that De Lorean and the company were guilty of many instances of fiscal malfeasance with British taxpayer money. Specifically the charges, or allegations as they soon came to be known, were that De Lorean had never invested personal funds promised; that money had been spent on "gold-plated faucets" in the company house in Belfast where, at the time, Bennington was living; that John had used government money to buy a $4.5 million estate in New Jersey; and that there were other instances of corporate misconduct both immoral and unethical, if not illegal.

Overnight the British press was on us like the proverbial cheap suit. My phone at home started ringing at 6 a.m. Saturday morning and only stopped ringing there when I was at work, where it rang constantly for the next two weeks. Haddad became a character in this play because the most damning piece of correspondence of all—the piece that was key to the entire list of allegations—was a memo from Bill to John that happened to list in succinct order every problem and potential problem that had ever faced the company in the realm of, guess what?, fiscal wrongdoing. The memo—I later saw the original when I was interviewed

by Scotland Yard in New York—was unsigned. Haddad said he sent it, De Lorean said he never received it, and indeed the original did not bear the stamp that was always put on all John's correspondence when it went through his secretary's hands. Of course not, Haddad said, it was too sensitive to be seen by his secretary, and had been placed on John's desk by Haddad himself. Ultimately, DMC was cleared of any wrongdoing by both the Scotland Yard investigation and the perusal of the books by government bean-counters in Belfast.

Marian? I haven't seen or heard from her since that Friday evening at the office.

The scandal? It had the British press, the British government and the De Lorean organization jumping for two weeks, spending valuable time and money on something other than the car business. It died down and then went away almost completely when the press got the scent of a much bigger story and one with some validity: the very real possibility the company might not survive.

Haddad, always the political creature, went on to run the fantastically successful primary and general election campaigns for Mario Cuomo in his quest to become governor of New York. Haddad is now involved in his favorite on-going struggle: the generic drug industry against the big drug houses.

The Speech Writer

I could never get a precise handle on another 43rd floor player. Maur Dubin was basically an interior decorator John's wife Cristina had picked up somewhere along the line. He decorated their Fifth Avenue apartment and could be found from time to time moving paintings and furniture around in the New York office. But I soon realized that Maur had moved beyond personal decorator and into the status of trusted friend, confidant and even advisor.

Haddad tells this story. He was assigned to get a speech written for De Lorean. Calling on his long association with the Washington, D.C., scene, Bill asked one of John Kennedy's speech writers to come up with the words. Bill gave the result to De Lorean one evening. The next morning John handed it back, saying, "Maur doesn't like it. Let's do something else."

Cristina's interior decorator didn't like a speech written by a man who used to write for the President of the United States.

At one particularly critical period when the memo scandal was raging at hurricane force, I was in De Lorean's office to give and get the latest confidential information. The survival of the company was in the balance. John and I were deep in some aspect of the problem when Maur Dubin strolled in, sat in John's easy chair and tuned in. My first reaction was to look at John for some sign, some indication to switch into a less confidential mode. When that didn't come I realized our interior decorator friend knew as much, perhaps more, about what was going on than I. Bizarre.

Cristina: Unequivocally Beautiful

No review of the 43rd floor personalities would be complete, of course, without mentioning Cristina. She is, simply, as nice a person as she is beautiful, and she is unequivocally one of the most beautiful women in the world. Despite her long involvement in the high-pressure, cut-throat, back-stabbing world of high fashion modeling, Cristina has managed, very deliberately, to remain innocent and unaffected. Her priorities are simple: John and the two children come first, then modeling.

She wasn't a full-time presence at the office, but was frequently there to visit John. During those periodic episodes of high drama—the memo scandal in particular—she was there more frequently, and when she wasn't there she would call me to find out what was going on because "John won't tell me. He doesn't want me to worry." And I, feeling very fatherly toward the boss's wife who also happened to be a Manhattan super star, would assure her that we were on top of the situation.

After the drug bust there was a good bit of criticism leveled at Cristina for being so blatant about bringing a designer in to create a "court room" wardrobe that would project the right image, and for publishing her diary of the immediate post-arrest events in *People* magazine.

I think both were ill-advised, but I also understand Cristina and why she did what she did. She knows clothes and understands the subtle and not so subtle messages clothing imparts. So a just-right wardrobe for John's court appearances and trial was a necessity. That reporters were watching her front door and would recognize the designer when he arrived would never occur to her. Along with maintaining her innocent and unaffected ways, Cristina has also managed to stay a bit immature, and what might seem obvious she would miss completely.

She can also be very headstrong when she gets the spirit. When the memo scandal broke, every reporter in town was trying to get through to us. I returned as many calls as I could, but couldn't get through to Jim Brady who writes a popular gossip column for the *New York Post*. That evening a rather damning Brady column ran telling the anti-De Lorean story. Cristina was pissed. She picked up the phone, called Brady and told him exactly what she thought of him and his column. Should have been disaster, but when it was all over, she had so charmed Brady with her forthrightness and obvious dedication to her husband his next column was as positive about De Lorean, and his wonderful wife, as the first had been negative.

An amazing lady.

Some Credit With The Blame

Because of the De Lorean Motor Co.'s total failure, it's easy to overlook some rather remarkable accomplishments. And while it wouldn't be accurate or fair to lay all the credit at De Lorean's feet, if he's going to carry the brunt of the responsibility for the terminal problems, let's at least credit him with creating an organization that has a lot about which to be proud.

If I was impressed with the quality of the personnel in the New York office, I was awed by the horsepower of the organization in Belfast. With the lure of pay and perks a good bit higher than the British and European auto industry was paying, and in many cases more importantly the opportunity to be a part of an exciting, pioneering project, De Lorean had pulled in some outstanding talent. It was needed, because the task was truly formidable. Not only did a brand new car have to be built, it had to be built in a manufacturing facility that had to be built.

We're a bit inured to the appearance of new models. General Motors and Ford and the others do it all the time. But they've been in business for quite a while; they have plants, personnel, engineering, design and development departments; they have long-term relationships with thousands of suppliers. De Lorean had nothing. Assembly line personnel had to be hired and trained, but first the hirers and trainers had to be hired and trained. The production process called for a lot of new machinery that had to be designed, built and installed. There were no parts bins filled with nuts and bolts and fasteners and all the doo-dads common to all cars that could be used in the New new De Lorean; all that had to be sourced, ordered and stocked, as did the parts unique to the car. Forget about the factory for a moment. The administrative department had to be filled with accountants and department heads and various specialists; they had to have secretaries and assistants and they all had to have offices filled with desks, chairs, typewriters, paper clips, staplers, stationery, envelopes, pencils and on and on and on.

Ground was broken in the cow pasture in Dunmurry outside Belfast in October, 1978. By January, 1981, the first official production car was completed. That's just 27 months from cows to cars and that accomplishment would not be out of place in the Guinness' Brothers book of records. Simply building a production facility in that amount of time is a worthy accomplishment. That the new plant was building a brand new car a few weeks later is little short of miraculous.

De Lorean himself spent little time in Belfast. Not only was he uncomfortable there—he feared for his safety I believe—his attitude seemed to be that he had hired the best men available and why should he stand around in the skeleton frame of a new plant looking at blueprints. His place, he reckoned, was back in New York (1) where it was safe and (2) where the financial community was headquartered.

Cafiero typically spent a week in N. Ireland and a week in New York. It was a crushing schedule, he admitted to me when he was leaving the company, and for whatever other reasons there may have been, it played a part in his going.

At the plant Cafiero worked with the first presi-

C.K. "Chuck" Bennington (left, with Gene Cafiero) headed plant operations as Managing Director of DMCL and established what would prove to be a disastrous policy of non-cooperation with the British press.
(Tony Howarth/Woodfin Camp & Associates)

dent or managing director of De Lorean Motor Co. Ltd., Charles "Chuck" Bennington, who came to DMCL from a long career in Chrysler's international operations. Bennington, thin, stern, bearded, and typically dressed in sport jacket and dark turtleneck, was dogmatic, unbending, unfriendly and, not surprisingly, unpopular among his key executives. He was not one of the people that impressed me. And at a time when it was essential the operation maintain good relations with the press—after all, we were spending millions of the taxpayers' dollars—he established a non-cooperation policy with the press that did, ultimately, irreparable harm.

When we should have been bringing the press in to show them and their readers what wonderful things were being done with all that money, Bennington kept everything wrapped in secrecy. Slowly the feeling that "if there's nothing to hide, why hide it?" was converted into strong suspicions, then accusations.

(An example: Tony Curtis, the editor of Britain's respected and popular *Motor* was kept waiting for an interview for five hours in Bennington's outer office. As a result, *Motor* became one of the operation's leading critics when it should have been made a strong ally.)

Bennington was replaced by Don Lander in the fall of 1980. Lander, another ex-Chrysler executive, was a 180-degree switch from Bennington, both personally and professionally. He brought a sense of order and direction to the operation that revived the enthusiasm for the long, grueling hours the task was requiring. Most of the executives worked 12 hours a day, seven days a week, and it takes more than salary and perks to keep up that pace. They were, and it's not trite to say it, dedicated.

Because of his quick in and out trips to N. Ireland and London, De Lorean exacerbated the company's poor press relations problem. He never gave himself the opportunity to let his immense charm work its magic on the press or, for that matter, on the important bureaucrats in the British government. In the U.S. his reputation was sound; that folk hero image lent credence and believability to everything he said and did. Not so in Britain. There he was known for his old playboy lifestyle. And traveling on the Concorde and staying at the Connaught did nothing to dispel the suspicion that the whole deal was designed to line his pockets, that the British taxpayer was going to be left with another Teapot Dome scandal. When the whole project began to unravel in the fall of 1981, when De Lorean desperately needed more money and concessions from the government, there was precious little support from the press or public to call on. Alan Watson, a reporter for the *Belfast Telegraph* and one of the few journalists who maintained an objective, even positive view, told one of my colleagues that winter just before the axe fell that the press and the majority of the public still felt that De Lorean was a "carpetbagger." Despite the plant, despite the car, despite the 2,800 employees, $180 million had gone away and they couldn't understand why. Or where.

Go To Plan B

The why and the where are not that difficult to fathom. When De Lorean was making what became his final plea to the British for money and export assistance, he admitted to me privately and later to the press that there had never been enough money, that the project was "undercapitalized from the start." Take that at face value, look no deeper, and you logically conclude the company ran out of money before it could make any. But simple logic would have dictated that if you don't get enough money to finance Plan A, you go to a less expensive Plan B, and you do that long before the tap has run dry. The scope of Plan A was simply too big right from the start—

too big a factory, too many employees, too many cars—and John had no intention of scaling down to a Plan B. He had a point to prove and he couldn't do it with 5,000 cars a year. When things were coming down around our ears—no money—Lander and the folks in Belfast were still working under De Lorean's last directive that had the factory gearing up to produce cars at an annual rate of some 30,000 a year. Based on our sales at the time, which were miniscule, we should have been at a rate of no more than 10,000 a year.

And Lander and his top executives had long since come to the conclusion that their biggest problem was the man himself. Over drinks at the Geneva Auto Show in the early spring of 1981—several months before the terminal problems set in—Lander, Barry Gill, and a couple of others agreed, in so many words, that if John would stay out of the British political situation and the running of the plant, they could put things on an even keel. He seemed unable to understand how the British thought, and why. He was constantly rubbing the bureaucrats the wrong way with statements and threats intended to get them to do what he wanted; specifically: give the company more money and export guarantees. The best thing that could happen to the company, they indicated, would be for John De Lorean to retire to his 43rd floor office and concentrate on his image making/perpetuating and leave the manufacturing of the cars and dealing with the government to the Belfast group.

Getting The Name Right

At the same time there was a similar, perhaps even stronger, feeling of the same nature out on the West Coast where C. R. "Dick" Brown was the executive in charge of the importing and distribution operation. Brown, yet another Chrysler alumnus, but more recently the man responsible for the temporarily successful introduction of Mazda into the U.S., was also rankling under De Lorean's giant presence.

Brown had joined De Lorean very early in the company's history; he was involved in recruiting the dealers in the original stock offering. Brown has a towering ego, which in itself is not out of place in the high pressure world of automobile wheeling and dealing. He is ruggedly handsome, perfectly coiffed, wears expensive suits, and carries with him an air of superiority as well as the aroma of 50 cent Garcia y Vega cigars. You can take the boy out of the country, etcetera. Autocratic and dogmatic, he was very difficult to work with and for.

Brown, while obsequious in De Lorean's presence, never missed an opportunity, with me at least, to reveal his displeasure with the way John was running the company. And he had the same disdain for Lander, Cafiero and especially Bruce McWilliams, the VP of marketing and advertising.

His complaints about De Lorean were never very specific, but seemed to generally revolve around De Lorean "not understanding" what was going on, setting unrealistic goals and making seemingly arbitrary decisions. While there was some truth to those charges, I believe Brown simply longed for complete autonomy; to build the De Lorean Motor Co. his way and to get credit for it. A popular line circulating through the California operation: "We're not building the De Lorean, it's the Brown. We just don't have the name right yet."

In no instance was that constant California vs. New York tension more evident than in Brown's relationship with Bruce McWilliams. As part of his longed-for autonomy, Brown wanted to not only have the company's advertising activities centered in Califor-

THE DMC-80: THE FUTURE BUS, TODAY

The DMC-80 is an Americanized version of the standard German bus which, on the streets of Hamburg in 1979, averaged 6.00 mpg. Even allowing for more rugged U.S. conditions, this far exceeds the U.S. fleet average for non-air conditioned buses.

The low floor and wide doors of the DMC-80 will provide rapid, effortless boarding and egress for all passengers, including the elderly. The addition of either a patented ramp or the newly developed front door lift will permit quick boarding by the handicapped.

This Americanized bus, when manufactured here in serial production, will be price-competitive with the buses now being sold in the United States.

The DMC-80 bus project siphoned off crucial time and dollars from the car, and was only abandoned in the fall of 1981 when DMC fortunes began to take a turn for the worse. (DMC)

nia, at an agency of his choice, but to also be in charge of it. But that's what De Lorean hired McWilliams to do. To say Brown made McWilliam's job difficult is an understatement. De Lorean would tell McWilliams to get on with some aspect of the advertising, McWilliams would try to coordinate it with Brown's marketing and sales requirements, Brown would say the plan shouldn't, wouldn't, couldn't work and would call De Lorean to convince him it was a bad plan or there was no money to support it, or both. De Lorean would back off and McWilliams would have to sit back and wait for the process to be repeated. As late as November of 1981 Brown, on the strength of thousands of deposits at dealerships, convinced De Lorean there was no need to do *any* advertising of any kind. When those deposits weren't converted into sales it was too late to crank up any meaningful advertising that could possibly have forstalled the impending disaster.

Although the three-headed beast De Lorean created—New York, California, Belfast—was unwieldy, it wasn't inherently impossible to control. But it demanded a very professional level of cooperation from all the players, and that we didn't get.

Buses, Skis And Smokey Yunick

Although my first responsibility on joining the company was the enthusiast press, my duties quickly expanded to include all aspects of our public relations efforts. There were a couple of major reasons for that. One, there had really been no public relations program and as we moved closer to production, and media interest increased we had to get things organized: press kits, photographs, product information, etc. and that task fell to me because of reason number two: Bill Haddad and his assistant, Dee Fensterer, were pursuing a non-related project, she full time, Bill perhaps 75 percent of his time. It was the De Lorean DMC

80, a bus to be built and sold to public transportation authorities. Buck Penrose also devoted a great deal of his time to the project developing the same kind of short- and long-term corporate plans he worked up for the car business.

The bus project fizzled out during the summer and fall of 1981 when everybody's energies had to be turned toward the car. And, I have to asssume, when funds to support the bus effort ran short. The bus project had no funding of its own as far as I could ever determine. Certainly the people working on it were on the DMC payroll.

John's ski slope grooming equipment manufacturing facility in Logan, Utah also came in for a good bit of attention by some of the staff, primarily Buck Penrose, with his gift for corporate planning and management, and Jim Season, the DMC assistant treasurer. Both were frequently in Logan. Although the sno-cats and groomers built there said De Lorean on them, they weren't gull-winged automobiles.

Smokey Yunick is many things. He's a legend in the stock car racing business as an "innovator," he's a brilliant automotive engineer/mechanic/developer, and he's a long-time close friend of John De Lorean. For several years Smokey has been working on a very fuel efficient version of the standard internal combustion engine that also promises tremendous horsepower production from very limited displacement. De Lorean was intrigued and began providing Smokey money for development. The goal was to build the engine for use in the De Lorean automobiles, but more importantly, John explained when I accompanied him on a trip to Smokey's Daytona Beach headquarters in October of 1981, the engine could be sold to other manufacturers and could be "bigger than the car company could ever be." Our involvement in that project went away at the first of the new year when, again, DMC was running out of money. British taxpayers' money.

159

Toasting the future at the ground-breaking for the factory in Northern Ireland. The date was October 2, 1978. (DMC)

Simple In The Asking

In the months following John's arrest I've been asked by everyone from a *Time* magazine reporter to the kid at the liquor store, "What do you think?" Simple in the asking, difficult in the answering. I think I still don't know what to think. Maybe when the trial is over, after a lot of unanswered questions have been answered, it will be easier to know what I think. I know what I feel. I feel sad. Those first few hours after the arrest produced some personally wrenching emotional moments: news film of that familiar figure, tieless, haggard, being led, handcuffed behind his back, into the court building in Los Angeles; the next day seeing him dressed in a dark blue short-sleeve prison jump suit, again handcuffed, climbing into a van to go to another court appearance. John De Lorean, handcuffed, riding in a prison van. I've ridden with him through London in a chauffeured Rolls Royce to buy a top coat at Burberry's and drop off a pair of custom-made shoes at Lobbs for resoleing. And when there wasn't news film to provide the images, I tried to imagine him sitting in a jail cell on Terminal Island. What was he doing, what was he thinking? I couldn't bring the image into focus. That cell was simply too far from the Connaught, too far from the Fifth Avenue apartment, too far from the office on the 43rd floor.

The dream he had, the dream that all of us who worked for him had, is gone.

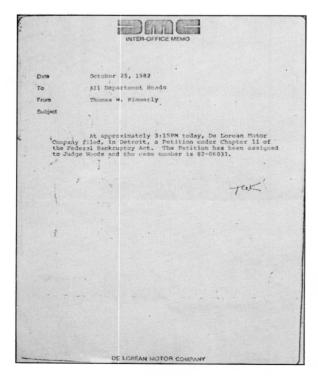

October 25, 1982. A bankruptcy notice for DMC is pinned to the door of the Irvine, California office. (Lamm)